T0346200

CAMBRIDGE KET

PRACTICE TESTS

for the Key English Test

Dorothy Adams

with Diane Flanel Piniaris

CENGAGE
Learning·

Australia · Brazil · Japan · Korea · Mexico · Singapore · Spain · United Kingdom · United States

Contents

Introduction

What makes this practice test book different from other test books available?

Cambridge KET Practice Tests is different because it is more than just a book of practice tests. It has been designed not only to familiarise students with the format and content of each part of the examination, but also to provide them with ample practice and further opportunity to develop the skills they need to succeed in the exam.

The book contains:

- 6 complete practice tests

- An In-depth Look and Exam Technique section for each paper (in Test One)

- 6 two-page Skills Spotlights (one after each test) designed to revise KET-level vocabulary, grammar and writing skills

- 6 Listening Spotlights (one after each Listening test) that provide extra listening practice and sharpen the skills students need to succeed in the Listening paper

- Helpful hints on how to approach each exercise type, including thorough guidance on writing tasks supported by model answers in the Teacher's Edition

The practice tests may be assigned for homework or done in class under timed conditions.

Cambridge Key English Test (KET): A brief outline of each paper

PAPER 1: READING AND WRITING (1 hour 10 minutes)

- **9 parts (56 items)**

    Part 1 – Matching: 5 items testing understanding of the gist of signs, notes, labels.

    Part 2 – Multiple-choice: 5 3-option items testing vocabulary related to a theme or simple story.

    Part 3 – Multiple-choice: 5 3-option items testing functional language in short dialogues. Candidates choose the correct response to an opening statement or question.

    Matching: extended dialogue in which one of the speaker's words are gapped. Candidates construct a continuous dialogue by choosing 5 out of 8 responses.

    Part 4 – Multiple-choice: 7 3-option items testing understanding of the main idea(s) and details of a longer text (about 230 words).

    Part 5 – Multiple-choice cloze: 8 3-option items testing structural elements (e.g., auxiliary verbs, modals, determiners, pronouns and prepositions).

    Part 6 – Word completion: 5 items testing vocabulary and spelling. Candidates must identify and spell words suggested by simple definitions; the initial letter of each word is given followed by a series of dashes that represent the missing letters.

    Part 7 – Open cloze: 1 or 2 short texts with 10 gaps testing structure and/or lexis.

    Part 8 – Information transfer: a 5-item fill-in exercise testing comprehension and accuracy. Candidates transfer information from 1 or 2 short input texts (e.g., an advert or letter) to an output text (e.g., a form or set of notes).

    Part 9 – Continuous writing: Candidates produce a short message, note or postcard (25 – 35 words) in response to a short input text asking for 3 discrete pieces of information.

All answers are written in pencil. Candidates indicate answers by shading lozenges (Parts 1 – 8) or writing answers (Part 9) on an answer sheet (see pages 146 – 147).

PAPER 2: LISTENING (approximately 30 minutes)

- **4 parts**   **Part 1 – Multiple-choice:** 5 three-picture items testing ability to identify key information in
  (25 items)   short monologues or dialogues. Candidates choose the picture that best answers the
             narrator's question.

             Part 2 – Matching: 5 items testing ability to identify key information in an extended informal
             dialogue. Candidates match the items to 8 options (e.g., people with places they
             want to visit).

             Part 3 – Multiple-choice: 5 3-option items testing ability to listen for key information in a
             neutral or informal dialogue.

             Part 4 – Gap-fill: 5 items testing ability to identify and interpret information in a neutral or
             informal dialogue. Candidates fill in one or more words or numbers on an order form
             or set of notes. Recognisable spelling is accepted, except for high-frequency words
             (e.g., *bus, red, days of the week*) or if spelling is dictated.

             Part 5 – Gap-fill: Same as part 4, except the listening text is a neutral or informal monologue.

Candidates hear each recording twice and write their answers in the test booklet. At the end of the test, they
are given 8 minutes to transfer their answers (in pencil) onto the answer sheet (see p. 148).

PAPER 3: SPEAKING (8 – 12 minutes)

Students are usually interviewed in pairs. Two examiners are present: one (the 'interlocutor') conducts the
interview and assesses; the second (the 'assessor') assesses, but does not take part in the conversation.

- **2 parts**   **Part 1 –** Short questions: Candidates respond to factual, personal questions from the examiner.

             Part 2 – Simulated situation: Candidates ask and answer questions using prompt cards.

Marking system

The three papers are weighted as follows: Paper 1: Reading and Writing counts for 50% of the final mark; Paper
2: Listening and Paper 3: Speaking count for 25% each of the final mark.

There is no individual pass mark for each paper.

Passing grades are **Pass** (about 70%) and **Pass with merit** (about 85%). Failing grades are **Narrow fail**
(within 5% of the pass mark) and **Fail**.

Each candidate receives a Statement of Results, which reports performance in each component as
'Exceptional', 'Good', 'Borderline' or 'Weak'.

For detailed information on how the writing task (question 56) and Speaking paper are marked, see pages 6 and 7.

On the day of the KET examination

The KET exam is usually available on fixed dates in March, May, June, November and December. Consult your
local Cambridge ESOL representative for precise details.

The written parts of the examination normally take place in the morning. The Speaking test is frequently
administered in the afternoon on the same day.

There is a short break between Paper 1 and Paper 2. There is also a break between the Listening paper and
the first scheduled Speaking test. Details of your Speaking test will be stated on the form you receive from your
local test administration centre.

Candidates need to take the following items with them to the examination centre:

- Statement of Entry/Timetable
- legal identification, such as an ID card or current passport
- pencils
- a pencil sharpener
- an eraser

Writing and Speaking criteria

Question 56 (short message)

This question is rated out of 5 marks. Answers are assessed according to the following mark scheme.

Marks	Criteria
5	All three parts of the message are clearly communicated. Only minor spelling errors or occasional grammatical errors are present.
4	All three parts of the message are communicated. Some errors in spelling, grammar and/or punctuation are present.
3	All three parts of the message are attempted. Expression may require interpretation by the reader. **OR** Two parts of the message are clearly communicated. Only minor spelling errors or occasional grammatical errors are present.
2	Only two parts of the message are communicated. Some errors in spelling and grammar are present. The errors in expression may require patience and interpretation by the reader.
1	Only one part of the message is communicated.
0	Question not attempted, or response is totally incomprehensible.

Assessment criteria for Paper 3: Speaking

General principles of assessment

- Candidates are assessed on their own individual performance and not in relation to each other.
- Candidates are assessed on their language skills, and not on their personality, intelligence or knowledge of the world.
- Candidates must be prepared to develop the conversation, where appropriate, and respond to set tasks.
- Candidates at KET level are not expected to produce completely accurate or fluent language, but they are expected to be able to interact appropriately and intelligibly with both the interlocutor and each other.
- Examiners expect the language resources and paraphrase strategies of most KET candidates to be limited but generally adequate to convey the intended meaning. Speech may sometimes be difficult to understand and there is hesitation, but generally appropriate interaction takes place.

Specific principles of assessment

- Paper 3 carries a total of 20 marks, which is scaled up to a mark out of 25. It represents 25% of the total score.
- Both examiners assess the candidates according to set criteria. The interlocutor (i.e., the examiner who conducts the interview) awards up to 5 marks for Global Achievement, while the second examiner (the assessor) awards up to 5 marks in each of the following areas: grammar and vocabulary; pronunciation; and interactive communication.

Here is a summary of what is assessed in each category:

AREA	WHAT IS ASSESSED
Global achievement (overall performance)	The candidate's overall effectiveness in dealing with both of the tasks (from the perspective of the interlocutor).
Grammar and vocabulary	The candidate's ability to use vocabulary, structure and paraphrase strategies to convey meaning. *Candidates at KET level are only expected to have limited linguistic resources. What is being assessed is the candidate's success in using these limited resources to communicate a message, rather than the range and accuracy of the candidate's grammar and vocabulary.*
Pronunciation	The intelligibility of the candidate's speech. *First-language interference is expected and is not penalised if it does not affect communication.*
Interactive communication	The candidate's ability to take part in the interaction appropriately. *Hesitation while the candidate searches for language is expected and is not penalised so long as it does not strain the patience of the listener. Candidates are given credit for being able to ask for repetition or clarification if necessary.*

An in-depth look

The paper has 9 parts.

PART 1 Questions 1 – 5 test your ability to understand short texts, such as signs and notices. It is a matching exercise consisting of 5 sentences and 8 signs/notices. You must match the signs/notices to the sentences that paraphrase them.

PART 2 Questions 6 – 10 test vocabulary. It is a multiple-choice exercise consisting of 5 items related to a theme or simple story line. Each gapped sentence is followed by 3 options (A, B and C). You must chose the option that completes the sentence.

PART 3 This part tests your ability to understand the language and logic of conversational exchanges. It is divided into 2 parts.

The first (questions 11 – 15) is a multiple-choice exercise with 5 short dialogues. Each dialogue contains a question or statement and 3 options (A, B and C). You must choose the option which best responds to the question or statement.

The second (questions 16 – 20) is a matching exercise in the form of an extended conversation between two friends. The second friend's responses are missing. You must complete the conversation by choosing responses from a list of 8 options (A – H).

PART 4 Questions 21 – 27 test your ability to understand a longer piece of writing. It is a multiple-choice exercise consisting of a passage (about 230 words) and five 3-option questions. There are two question types: choose the answer from 3 options (A, B and C), or decide whether each statement is Right (A), Wrong (B) or Doesn't Say (C), if the information is not in the passage.

PART 5 Questions 28 – 35 test your knowledge of grammar, structure and usage. It is a multiple-choice cloze passage with 8 gaps. You must fill in each gap by choosing the best word from 3 options (A, B and C).

PART 6 Questions 36 – 40 test vocabulary and spelling. It is a word-completion exercise. Each of the items is a dictionary-style definition related to a theme (e.g., jobs, food or leisure activities). You must write the word which is defined. The first letter is given, along with a set of dashes representing the remaining letters. A mark is awarded for each correctly spelt word.

PART 7 Questions 41 – 50 test structure and vocabulary. It is an open cloze exercise consisting of 1 or 2 short texts with 10 gaps (for example, e-mails or postcards). You must complete each gap with 1 word. To receive a mark, the word must be correctly spelt.

PART 8 Questions 51 – 55 test your ability to understand and extract factual information from 1 or 2 short texts (e.g., an advertisement, post-it note or letter). It is an information transfer exercise. You must use information in the texts to complete 5 gaps in an order form, notice or similar document. To do well, you must understand language associated with forms (e.g., *surname* and *date of birth*). To receive a mark, the answers must be correctly spelt and, where necessary, capitalised.

PART 9 Question 56 tests your ability to write a short message (25 – 35 words) in response to a short written text (e.g., an e-mail, message or letter). The text you reply to contains 3 questions, which you must answer in your response. Spelling and grammar are important in this part.

Marking and answer sheet

Paper 1 is worth 60 marks. Questions 1 – 55 are worth 1 mark, and question 56 is marked out of 5. (For information on the criteria for marking question 56, see page 6.)

Paper 1 counts for 50% of your final mark.

You must write your answers in pencil on the answer sheet (see pages 146 – 147). You will not be given extra time to transfer your answers onto the answer sheet.

Exam technique

Manage your time carefully.

You have 1 hour and 10 minutes for the Reading and Writing Paper. This means that it's important to manage your time carefully. If you don't, you won't have enough time to answer all the questions.

Here is a suggested plan:

PART	ITEMS/TASK TYPE	SUGGESTED
1	5 items: matching text + signs	3 minutes
2	5 items: multiple-choice vocabulary	3 minutes
3	10 items: dialogues (short and extended)	10 minutes
4	7 items: multiple-choice reading task	10 minutes
5	8 items: multiple-choice cloze passage	10 minutes
6	5 items: word completion	3 minutes
7	10 items: open cloze passage	6 minutes
8	5 items: information transfer	10 minutes
9	Writing task - question 56 (5 marks)	15 minutes

Think about it: 3 minutes to do 5 items in Parts 1, 2, and 6 sounds like a short time, but it actually gives you 40 seconds per item, which is more than enough time to answer a one-sentence question. Try this item from a typical Part 2 and see for yourself. Ask your teacher to time you, and see how long it takes. Record your time on the line at the right.

Rita was .... a lovely new skirt yesterday.

A putting   (B) wearing   **C** dressing   _____ seconds

Don't spend too much time on any one question.

This is the key to careful time management. If you're not sure of an answer, admit you're not sure, guess ... and then move on! You don't lose marks for wrong answers, so you have nothing to lose (and everything to gain) by guessing.

Your goal should be to get through every question ... and then when you finish, you can go back and spend time checking your work and thinking about questions you weren't sure of.

TIP: Try putting a light pencil mark in the exam booklet next to questions that you're unsure of. If you get through all the questions before time is up, look back through the exam paper and spend more time on the questions you've marked.

Leave plenty of time to plan, write and check the writing task in Part 9 (question 56).

Question 56 is a writing task worth 5 marks, so it's important that you spend more time on it.

Remember that accurate spelling and grammar are important in this task, so make sure that you leave yourself time to read over your work.

Keep track of your test times, and find your own rhythm.

The timings suggested in the table above are only a rough guide. As you do each Paper 1 in this book, keep a record of your time for each section, and find a formula that works for you.

Remember: The important thing is to have a plan when you go into the exam ... and then stick to it when the clock begins to tick!

Part 1

Questions 1 – 5

Which notice (**A – H**) says this (**1 – 5**)?

For questions **1 – 5**, mark the correct letter **A – H** on your answer sheet.

Example:

0   ...F....   It is unsafe to walk here.

Answer:

0	A	B	C	D	E	F	G	H
	▭	▭	▭	▭	▭	▬	▭	▭

1   ...D...   You must not park your car here.

A   **Spend over £50 and enter prize draw.**

2   ...C...   Students can buy things for less money.

B   **CHILDREN'S CLOTHING** First Floor

3   ...E...   Only people who work here can park in this area.

C   **20% discount for students**

4   ...A...   Anyone who spends more than £50 could win a prize.

D   **NO PARKING**

5   ...G...   You cannot enter the building through this door.

E   **EMPLOYEES' CAR PARK**

F   **DANGER!** WET FLOOR

G   **EXIT ONLY**

H   **STUDENT LOAN OFFICE**

Tip

Always underline key words in sentences 1 – 5. Then find words and phrases in the signs that are similar in meaning.

TRY IT! - Write the words or phrases from signs A – H that mean the same as these words from sentences 1 – 5. The first is done as an example.

0   It is unsafe - ....danger.........
1   must not park - ....no parking......
2   buy things for less money - ......discount......
3   people who work here - ....employees....
4   more than - ....over.........
5   cannot enter - ......exit (only)....

THINK ABOUT IT! - Sometimes a sentence contains 'not' + the opposite of a word or phrase in the sign. Which item in this exercise does this? ....5.........

Part 2

Questions 6 – 10

Read the sentences about families.
Choose the best word (**A**, **B** or **C**) for each space.

For questions **6 – 10**, mark **A**, **B** or **C** on your answer sheet.

Example:

0 John's brother .... 12 years old.

    (**A**) is   **B** has   **C** are

Answer:

---

6 My cousin Mary is married .... a man called Simon.

    (**A**) to   **B** with   **C** from

7 Everyone says that I look .... my father.

    A same   **B** as   (**C**) like

8 We .... my grandparents last weekend.

    A went   (**B**) visited   **C** travelled

9 I hate it when my sister .... my clothes.

    A lends   (**B**) borrows   **C** puts

10 My mother gets upset when I .... a mess in my room.

    (**A**) make   **B** do   **C** be

Tip

Part 2 tests vocabulary, structure and meaning. Make sure that the word you choose fits with the words before and after the gap.

TRY IT! - Look at the example in Part 2 again. Answer the questions.

1 Which 2 choices could come after the phrase 'John's brother ...'? ....A, B...........

2 Now look at the whole sentence. Which choice no longer fits? ....B...........

3 Why? In English, we express age with the verb 'be', not with 'have'.

Part 3

Questions 11 – 15

Complete the five conversations.

For questions **11 – 15**, mark **A, B** or **C** on your answer sheet.

Example:

0

What do you do in your free time?

A I listen to music.

B The cinema.

C At weekends.

Answer:

0	A	B	C

11 Shall we go to the disco tomorrow night?

    A Not very often
    (B) Great idea!
    C Every Saturday.

12 Do you like Italian food?

    (A) Yes, it's my favourite.
    B I do, too.
    C Yes, I'd like to try it.

13 What's your favourite colour?

    A I haven't got anyone.
    (B) It's red.
    C I don't like one.

14 Why are you late?

    (A) I missed the bus.
    B An hour ago.
    C I'll come later.

15 When's Mary's birthday?

    A Two weeks ago.
    B It's last week.
    (C) It's next week.

Tip

How to approach questions 11 – 15

Always focus carefully on what the first speaker says, and think about the following:

- Is it a **yes/no question** beginning with an auxiliary verb like *do, did, have, can,* etc.?
  If so, the answer will probably begin with *Yes* or *No* or be a sentence where *yes* or *no* is understood.
- Is it an **information question**?
  If so, underline the *wh-* word and think carefully about what information the first speaker is asking for.
  For example, *when* requires an answer with a time expression, *where* requires a place, *why* requires a reason or explanation.
- Is it an **invitation** ('Shall we go to the cinema tonight?')? A **suggestion** ('Let's call Mike.')? An **offer** ('Would you like a cup of coffee?')? A **request** ('Could you lend me the car tonight?')?
  If so, look for an option that expresses acceptance or rejection of the idea: for example, 'Good idea!' - 'Sorry, I'm too tired.' - 'I'd love one.' - 'Sorry, I need it.'

Questions 16 – 20

Complete the conversation.
What does Lenny say to Amy?

For questions **16 – 20**, mark the correct letter **A – H** on your answer sheet.

Example:

Amy: How do you like your new language school?

Lenny: **0** ....*B*....   *Answer:*

Amy: Have you made any friends there yet?

Lenny: **16** ....D....

Amy: Where's he from?

Lenny: **17** ....F....

Amy: I'd like to meet him. I know! Why don't we all go for a coffee this afternoon?

Lenny: **18** ....C....

Amy: Let's go to Café Espresso on Bridge Street.

Lenny: **19** ....A....

Amy: How about after your lesson at 4 o'clock?

Lenny: **20** ....H....

Amy: Great! I'm looking forward to it.

A   Yes, I'm sure he'll like it there. What time shall we meet?

B   It's great, and the teachers are really friendly.

C   I'd like that. Where shall we go?

D   Yes, a lot, but my best friend is Heinrich.

E   It's a bit too late.

F   He's from Germany.

G   It's a big building with a park.

H   Good idea! See you later.

Tip

How to approach the extended dialogue

- First, read the dialogue without worrying about the gaps. Then read the options. This will give you an idea of the overall meaning and the kind of information that is missing in each gap.
- Remember to cross out the option that fits in '0' so you don't re-use it!
- Next, work through the dialogue slowly. Underline key words, then go through the options one by one to find a suitable response.
- Make sure the option you choose fits with what goes after it, as well as what goes before it.
- When you finish, read through the completed dialogue to see if it makes sense.

Part 4

Questions 21 – 27

Read the article about a hen called Daisy.
Are sentences **21 – 27** 'Right' (**A**) or 'Wrong' (**B**)?
If there is not enough information to answer 'Right' (**A**) or 'Wrong' (**B**), choose 'Doesn't say' (**C**).

For questions **21 – 27**, mark **A**, **B** or **C** on your answer sheet.

Hen Friend

When Julie Carver was six years old, she lived on a farm. It was her job to feed the hens every morning before breakfast. There were three hens: Daisy, Maisie and Lazy. Daisy was Julie's favourite. Every day when Julie came home from school, Daisy ran to the gate, flapping her wings and squawking loudly.

One day Julie was feeling ill and couldn't go to school. Daisy sat outside the house all day making the 'koor, koor' sound that hens make when their chicks are young.

When Julie was nine, her father got a new job. The family left the farm and went to live in a flat in town. They couldn't take the hens with them. Julie was sad. The people who bought their farm promised to take good care of the hens, but Julie knew she was going to miss Daisy.

One day Julie's teacher decided to take the class on a picnic. The picnic was in a park near Julie's old home. Julie was sitting with her friends, enjoying herself. Suddenly, they heard a loud squawking noise. They looked up and saw a hen running towards them, flapping its wings. It was Daisy!

When the picnic ended, Julie took Daisy back to the farm. The new owners invited her to visit Daisy at weekends and during the school holidays. Daisy and Julie were very happy.

Example:

0	Julie woke up at 6 o'clock every morning.							

0 Julie woke up at 6 o'clock every morning.

A Right   **B** Wrong   Ⓒ Doesn't say   *Answer:* | 0 | A ▭   B ▭   C ▬ |

---

21 There were three hens on the farm where Julie lived.

Ⓐ Right   **B** Wrong   **C** Doesn't say

22 There were many other animals on Julie's farm.

A Right   **B** Wrong   Ⓒ Doesn't say

23 Daisy met Julie outside school every day.

A Right   Ⓑ Wrong   **C** Doesn't say

24 Julie went on a picnic with her family.

A Right   Ⓑ Wrong   **C** Doesn't say

25 The park was near the farm where Julie lived when she was younger.

Ⓐ Right   **B** Wrong   **C** Doesn't say

26 Julie's friends liked Daisy.

A Right   **B** Wrong   Ⓒ Doesn't say

27 Julie is going to spend some of her free time with Daisy.

Ⓐ Right   **B** Wrong   **C** Doesn't say

Tip

Right, Wrong or Doesn't Say

In this task type you must decide whether an answer is 'right', 'wrong' or 'doesn't say'. Sometimes KET candidates get confused between 'wrong' and 'doesn't say'. Let's look at question 22 to show you the difference.

You know from answering question 21 that paragraph 1 talks about the hens on Julie's farm. To decide whether the statement in question 22 is 'right', 'wrong' or 'doesn't say', read through the next few lines and ask yourself: 'Does the writer mention any other animals'? (Remember that the questions follow the order of the text, so the information should come early in the passage.) If no other animals are mentioned, then the answer is 'doesn't say'. If the answer is 'wrong', then you would expect to find a sentence like 'There were only a few other animals on the farm' or 'There was also a pig on the farm'.

Part 5

Questions 28 – 35

Read the article about part-time jobs.
Choose the best word (**A**, **B**, or **C** for each space.)

For questions **28 – 35**, mark **A**, **B** or **C** on your answer sheet.

Teenagers at Work

What can you do if you want to buy **(0)** .... new mobile phone or some new clothes **(28)** .... you don't have any money? Well, if you live **(29)** .... Britain, you can get a part-time job.

If you are 13 or 14, you can get a 'paper round' and deliver newspapers to people's homes, like Kelly Sales. 'You **(30)** .... to get up at 6 am every morning, and it takes about 45 minutes to deliver all the papers,' says Kelly. 'Most days I love my paper round, but not when it rains. It's **(31)** .... to fold the papers and put them **(32)** .... a letterbox when you're holding an umbrella!'

If you are 15 or older, you **(33)** .... work in a shop for up to eight hours on Saturdays. A lot of teenagers work in their **(34)** .... clothes shop or music shop. Most shops will also let you work during the school holidays. 'I'm really looking forward to being 15,' says Kelly, '**(35)** .... my aunt has a brilliant clothes shop and she's offered me a Saturday job there.'

Example:

| 0 | **A** the | **B** a | **C** an | *Answer:* | 0 | A ▭ | B ▬ | C ▭ |

28	**A** or	**B** so	**C** but
29	**A** at	**B** in	**C** to
30	**A** have	**B** should	**C** must
31	**A** hardest	**B** hardly	**C** hard
32	**A** in	**B** under	**C** to
33	**A** shall	**B** would	**C** can
34	**A** popular	**B** famous	**C** favourite
35	**A** so	**B** because	**C** but

Tip

How to approach Part 5

- Read the text first without worrying about the missing words. This helps you to get a feel for the overall meaning of the text.
- Then go back and work on the missing words. Think about what is missing: a preposition? a modal verb? a linking word? an adjective? a gerund?
- To check yourself, read the passage again. Ask yourself questions like: Does each choice fit grammatically into the sentence? Are the verbs in the right tenses? Do my choices fit the meaning of the text?

Mind the gap!
It's important to check that the answer you select fits with what follows the gap, as well as with what comes before it. Look at gap 30. All 3 choices fit with what goes before the gap, but the gap is followed by the word 'to'. That leaves only one possible answer, as both *should* and *must* are followed by the base form of a verb.

Part 6

Questions 36 – 40

Read the descriptions of some things you might find in a sports centre.
What is the word for each one?

The first letter is already there. There is one space for each other letter in the word.

For questions **36 – 40**, write the words on your answer sheet.

Example:

| 0 | This is a word for all the things you use when you play a sport. | e q u i p m e n t |

Answer: | **0** | equipment |

| 36 | You can come here to swim. | p o o l |

| 37 | This is something you use to get dry. | t o w e l |

| 38 | This is a loose comfortable outfit you wear when you exercise. | t r a c k s u i t |

| 39 | You hit the ball with this when you play tennis. | r a c q u e t |

| 40 | These are the special shoes you wear in a sports centre. | t r a i n e r s |

Tip

Singular or plural?
Read each question carefully to see whether you need to spell the singular or plural form of the word.

THINK ABOUT IT! - How can you tell whether an answer needs to be singular or plural? Look for clues in the definitions. Words and phrases like *this is*, *it's* and *here* (i.e., in this place) require a singular noun; *these are / they're* require a plural answer.

TRY IT! - Look at questions 36 – 40. Is the answer singular or plural? Underline the words that tell you.
Questions 0, 36, 37, 38 and 39 are singular. Question 40 is plural.

Part 7

Questions 41 – 50

Complete these e-mails.
Write ONE word for each space.

For questions **41 – 50**, write the words on your answer sheet.

Example: | **0** | *my*

Hi, Sarah,

I can't find (0) ....*my*....... English book. I think (41) ....I......... left it (42) ....at........ your house (43) ....on........ Saturday morning. Can you look (44) ....for........ it, please? My exams start on Monday, (45) ......and...... the first one is English.

Thanks,

Jenny

Dear Jenny,

Sorry I didn't reply sooner, but I had a problem (46) ......with...... my computer. Don't worry. I found your book. It was next to (47) ......the...... phone. I think you left it there (48) ......when...... you phoned your mum. I've (49) ....got....... to stay home and study today, (50) ....but....... I can ask my dad to bring it to you.

Good luck with your exams.

Sarah

Tip

How to approach Part 7

- Read the text(s) without worrying about the missing words. This helps you to get a feel for the overall meaning and context.
- Then go back and work on each missing word. Think about what is missing: a preposition? a past participle or modal verb? a linking word like *and, but* or *when*? a possessive adjective like *my* or *yours*? an article like *a, an* or *the*?
- To check yourself, read the text(s) again. Ask yourself questions like: Does each choice fit grammatically into the sentence? Are the verbs in the right tenses? Do my choices fit the meaning of the text?
- **Remember:** Correct spelling is essential in this part of the test.

Part 8

Questions 51 – 55

Read the information about buying flowers.
Complete Wendy's notes.

For questions **51 – 55**, write the information on your answer sheet.

FLOWERS BY E-MAIL

Special offers:

♦ 12 red roses only £10

♦ 24 assorted flowers £15

Offer available to end of month.

When you order, please tell us whether you would like a red, blue, orange or pink ribbon.

Free delivery.

Credit card payment only.

orders@flowersbyemail.co.uk.

Wendy,

It's Mother's Day next week.

Would you mind ordering Mum some flowers for me? The offer says you can only pay by credit card, and I haven't got one.

I'd like 24 assorted flowers with a red ribbon. Please ask them to send them to Mum's address:

17 Walford Lane

Thanks,

Vera

WENDY'S NOTES

Special occasion:		Mother's Day
Kind of flowers:	**51**	assorted
Number of flowers:	**52**	24
Colour of ribbon:	**53**	red
Price:	**54**	£15 / fifteen pounds
Address:	**55**	17 Walford Lane

Tip

In this task you often have to consider information in both texts to find the answer to a question. For example, question 51 asks you to fill in the 'kind of flowers'. In the advertisement, there are two types of flowers on offer: red roses and assorted flowers. You need to read the second note to find out what kind of flowers Vera wants her friend to order.

Remember: Correct spelling is essential in this part of the exam. Always look back at the text(s) to check the spelling of your answers.

Part 9

Question 56

Read this note from your English pen-friend, David.

Dear .... ,

Here are some photographs of my family. Please send me some photographs of your family. How many brothers and sisters have you got? What are their names? How old are they?

Write soon,
David

Write David a note. Answer the questions.

Write **25 – 35** words.

Write the letter on your answer sheet.

Tip

Before you begin, list the points you must write about:

1 How many brothers/sisters have I got?
2 What are their names?
3 How old are they?

Use this list to check your answer:

Have you ...

• thanked David for the photographs?

• written about all 3 points?

• used a closing phrase such as 'Regards' or 'Best wishes'?

• signed your name?

• proofread for grammar, spelling and punctuation?

• checked your word count?

QUESTION 56: MODEL ANSWER

Dear David,

Thanks for the photographs. I like them very much. Here are some photographs of my family. I have one brother. His name is Carlos. He is 15 years old.

Regards,
Julio

33 words

An in-depth look

Paper 2: Listening takes about 30 minutes, including 8 minutes at the end to transfer your answers onto the answer sheet.

Paper 2 has five parts. <u>You will hear each part twice.</u>

PART 1 Questions 1 – 5 test your ability to listen for factual information (times, prices, days of the week, etc.). It is an illustrated multiple-choice exercise. Each item you hear contains a narrator's question and a short dialogue (e.g., a conversation between two friends or between a customer and a shop assistant). In your test booklet, you will see a question and 3 pictures for each item. As you listen, you must choose the picture (A, B or C) that best represents the answer to the question.

PART 2 Questions 6 – 10 test your ability to listen for factual information in a longer informal dialogue between two people who know each other. It is a matching exercise with 5 items and 8 options. You must match the items with the options: e.g., people with places they would like to visit or days of the week with the activities that someone does on those days. Typical topics are: daily life, travel and free-time activities.

PART 3 Questions 11 – 15 also test your ability to listen for factual information. It is a 3-option multiple-choice exercise based on a longer dialogue. Sometimes the dialogue is between friends who are discussing a topic of personal interest to them; sometimes it is between people doing business with each other (e.g., a customer and a travel agent or a tour guide and a tourist).

PARTS Questions 16 – 25 test your ability to listen for factual information from a dialogue or monologue.
4 / 5 Both tasks are gap-filling exercises that require you to write down information based on what you hear. The information could be numbers, times, dates, prices, names, addresses and so on. Incorrect spelling is acceptable in this part, except for high-frequency words or words which are spelt out in the recording.

Marking and answer sheet

There are 25 questions in Paper 2. Each question is worth 1 mark.

Paper 2 counts for 25% of your final mark.

Unlike Paper 1 (where you mark your answers directly onto the answer sheet), in the Listening paper you are instructed to first mark your answers in the test booklet. At the end of Part 5, you will be given 8 minutes to transfer your answers in pencil onto the Paper 2 answer sheet (see page 148).

Exam technique

During the test

- Look at the questions *before* you listen. This will help you to decide what you need to listen for.

- Don't worry if you hear any unfamiliar words. If you focus on the *general* meaning of what you hear, you will still be able to answer most of the questions.

- Remember that you will hear each item twice. Answer as many questions as you can the first time you listen. Use the second time to check your answers and complete anything you did not answer on the first listening.

- Answer *all* the questions. You won't lose marks for wrong answers, so if you don't know the answer, guess.

At the end of the test

- You have 8 minutes to transfer your answers from your test booklet onto the Paper 2 answer sheet.

- As you transfer each answer, check that you have placed it next to the correct question number on your answer sheet.

Part 1

Questions 1 – 5

You will hear five short conversations.
You will hear each conversation twice.
There is one question for each conversation.
For questions **1 – 5**, put a tick (✔) under the right answer.

Example:

0   How many students are there in the language class?

9	10	15
A ✔	B ☐	C ☐

1   What is the man going to drink?

A ☐   B ☐   C ✔

2   What did the woman and her husband do on Friday?

A ✔   B ☐   C ☐

3 Where did the teacher spend last summer?

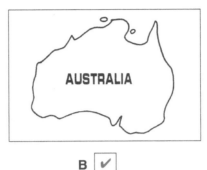

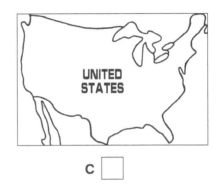

A ☐

B ✔

C ☐

4 Which subject does the man prefer?

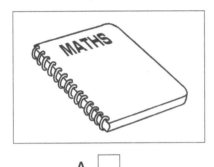

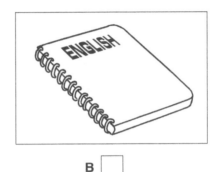

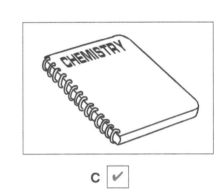

A ☐

B ☐

C ✔

5 Which shop will they go to next?

A ✔

B ☐

C ☐

Tip

- Always read the questions before the recording is played.
- Underline or circle the question word in each item: e.g., *what, where, when, which, how, how much*. This will help you focus on what to listen for.
- Pay attention to *who* each question asks about: the man, the woman or both. In question 4, for example, if you do not realise that the question asks about the man, you might choose option B, 'English', which is the subject the woman says she likes best.
- If time allows, study the pictures. What do they show? How are they similar/different? The speakers will usually mention something related to each picture, so looking at the pictures first helps to prepare you for what you will hear.

Part 2

Questions 6 – 10

Listen to Donna talking to Henry about painting her new flat.
What colours is Donna going to use?

For questions **6 – 10**, write a letter (**A – H**) next to each part of the flat.
You will hear the conversation twice.

Example:

0	bathroom	*H*

Parts of the Flat

6	hall	C
7	front door	B
8	kitchen	A
9	dining room	D
10	ceilings	G

Colours

A	blue
B	brown
C	cream
D	green
E	grey
F	red
G	white
H	yellow

Tip

Before you listen ...
- Always read the words in the left-hand column so you know what to listen for.

As you listen ...
- Be careful not to answer too quickly. You may hear one of the speakers mention a choice on the right, but don't assume it's always the right answer. Often the speakers introduce new information as the dialogue continues.

  An example of this is item (0). First, you hear the woman say, 'The bath, sink and toilet are green ...', which might make you choose option D. But then she says, '... so I'm going to paint the walls yellow.' This means the right answer is 'H', and not 'D'.

Part 3

Questions 11 – 15

Listen to Dawn asking about English Homestead Courses.

For questions **11 – 15**, tick (✔) **A, B** or **C**.
You will hear the conversation twice.

Example:

0	Students on an English Homestead Course stay	A	in a school.	☐
		B	in their teacher's home.	✔
		C	in a college.	☐

11	Last Saturday the students went	A	to London.	✔
		B	to the sports centre.	☐
		C	to the cinema.	☐

12	The only book the students have to take with them is	A	a dictionary.	✔
		B	a course book.	☐
		C	a grammar practice book.	☐

13	Most of the courses are	A	in Scotland.	☐
		B	in Wales.	☐
		C	in England.	✔

14	A one-week course costs	A	£250.	✔
		B	£215.	☐
		C	£860.	☐

15	The only thing that students have to pay extra for is	A	meals.	☐
		B	accommodation.	☐
		C	excursions.	✔

Tip

Before you listen ...
• Read the instructions and questions before you listen. If time allows, also read the options. This gives you a good idea of what the passage is about. It also helps you identify the details you must listen for.

As you listen ...
• Don't tick an option just because you hear it! Remember that the speaker will usually mention all three options, so you need to listen carefully to pick out the right answer to the question.

For example, in the part of the dialogue that relates to item (0), the speaker mentions 'school', 'teacher's home' and 'college', but what he says is 'You *don't* go to a school or college. You stay in your English teacher's home.' So the correct answer is 'B'.

Part 4

Questions 16 – 20

You will hear a man booking a table at a restaurant.

Listen and complete questions **16 – 20**.
You will hear the conversation twice.

GINO'S RESTAURANT
Booking Form

Occasion: *Mother's birthday*

Day and date:

16	.......*Friday*....... , *20 May*

Number of people:

17	6 / six

Time:

18	7 / seven o'clock

Words on cake:

19	Happy Birthday

Name:

20	*Nick* ...*Sherman*...

Tip

Parts 4 and 5

Before you listen ...

- Always look at the items that you must fill in *before* you listen. These tell you exactly what information you must listen for: e.g., date, time, price, address.

As you listen ...

- If one of the answers is a name or an address, be prepared to hear one of the speakers spell it out to the person he or she is speaking to. You need to spell such items correctly or you will not be given a mark for them.

Part 5

Questions 21 – 25

You will hear some information about the Eastern Link Bus Service.

Listen and complete questions **21 – 25**.
You will hear the information twice.

Eastern Link Bus Service

Travel from home to:	shops and local coach and train stations
Cost of single journey:	**21** £ .1.50............
Cost of return journey:	**22** £ .2.50............
To book a seat, phone:	**23** 0880 233 1888
Recommended booking time:	**24** at least ....2 hours..... before travelling
Address of office:	**25** 50 Station Road

You now have 8 minutes to write your answers on the answer sheet.

Listening Spotlight 1

Audioscript on page 157.

In Part 4 of the Listening Paper, one of the speakers may spell out a word. It is important that you spell such words correctly. This exercise helps you to revise the letters of the alphabet.

Listen to a man talking to a travel agent. For items 1 – 8, write the words the man spells.

1	..........Campbell..........	5	44 ....Judgement Way..........
2	..........Graham..........	6	..........Exeter..........
3	..........Yvonne..........	7	..........EQ1 4FK..........
4	..........Elizabeth..........	8	..........Didcot..........

An in-depth look

Paper 3: Speaking lasts 8 to 10 minutes. Usually two candidates are examined by two examiners; if you are in the last session you may be one of three candidates. During the exam, one of the examiners (the interlocutor) speaks to the candidates and explains the tasks, while the other examiner (the assessor) listens. At the end, both examiners assess your performance.

The Speaking paper has two parts. Part 1 lasts 5 – 6 minutes and Part 2 lasts 3 – 4 minutes.

PART 1 tests your ability to give information about yourself (for example, where you live, your interests, your studies, your likes and dislikes). Both candidates have a short conversation with the examiner.

PART 2 tests your ability to interact in English by asking and answering questions about places, times, services, where to go, how to get to places and what to eat. In the first phase of the activity, the examiner gives one candidate a prompt card with information about an event, a contest, a place of interest, etc. The other candidate receives a card with question prompts. You then proceed to ask and answer questions based on the cards you have been given. In the second phase, you will reverse roles.

Marking

Paper 3 is worth 25 marks.

It counts for 25% of your final mark.

You will get a mark from 1 – 5 for each of the following categories:

- **Overall performance:** how well you have dealt with all of the tasks.

- **Grammar and vocabulary:** your ability to use grammar and vocabulary sufficiently well to communicate your message.

- **Pronunciation:** your ability to pronounce English words clearly enough to be understood.

- **Interactive communication:** your ability to communicate with both the examiner and the other candidate. You will also be given credit for being able to ask your partner or the examiner to repeat or clarify information if necessary.

Your mark is then changed into a mark out of 25.

For more information on KET Speaking criteria, see page 7.

Exam technique

Before the exam

It is natural for candidates to be nervous before the KET Speaking test. Here are some ideas to help you relax:

* Take several deep breaths before you go into the room.

* Look at the examiners and smile. This will help everyone feel more relaxed.

* Take a few seconds to get comfortable in your chair.

* Remember that the examiners are used to talking to candidates with trembling hands and shaky voices. They expect you to be nervous, and it's part of their job to help you feel more relaxed and comfortable.

When the exam begins

Here is what you can expect to hear from the lead examiner when you enter the room:

> **Examiner:** *Good morning/afternoon/evening.*
> *Can I have your mark sheets, please?*

Next, the examiner will introduce himself/herself and the second examiner.

> **Examiner:** *I'm* .... [says name], *and this is* .... [introduces second examiner].
> *He/She is just going to listen to us.*

After that, the examiner will ask you and your partner your names. Be prepared to spell your surname, using English letters (for example, 'My surname is Smith. That's S – M – I – T – H .').

Part 1 (5 – 6 minutes)

Questions for Both Candidates

What's your name?
What's your surname?
How do you spell that?
Where do you come from?

Do you work or are you a student?
What do you do/study?
Do you like it?
Why?/Why not?

Questions for Candidate A

Do you go to the theatre often?
What sort of music do you like?
Have you got any brothers or sisters?
Tell me something about the food you like.

Questions for Candidate B

Have you visited any other towns in your country?
What are you going to do next weekend?
How often do you watch TV?
Tell me something about your home town.

Part 2 (3 – 4 minutes)

1   Candidate A, here is some information about a School Sports Day.

Candidate B, you don't know anything about the School Sports Day, so ask A some questions about it. Now B, ask A your questions about the School Sports Day and A, you answer them.

[Candidate A looks at Prompt Card 1A on next page]
[Candidate B looks at Prompt Card 1B on next page]

2   Candidate B, here is some information about a Hi-Tech Exhibition.

Candidate A, you don't know anything about the Hi-Tech Exhibition, so ask B some questions about it. Now A, ask B your questions about the Hi-Tech Exhibition and B, you answer them.

[Candidate B looks at Prompt Card 2A on next page]
[Candidate A looks at Prompt Card 2B on next page]

Tip

- Listen carefully when the examiner speaks. If you don't understand a question, ask the examiner to repeat it. (Remember to say 'please'; it always creates a good impression.)

- Don't forget to look at the examiner when you speak. It will make you seem more confident.

Frequently Asked Questions: Speaking (Part 1)

- **What if the examiner asks me about my hobbies and interests, but I don't have any hobbies or interests?**
  Be honest. If you don't have any hobbies or interests, or you don't like any of the subjects you are studying, don't be afraid to say so. Remember that the examiners are marking you on how well you speak, and not on your hobbies or your opinions about education or work.

- **Will I get a better mark if I use a lot of idioms, expressions and advanced vocabulary?**
  Only if you feel comfortable using them. This is not a vocabulary test. Your goal is to sound as natural and fluent as possible, and you can do that with simpler language that you feel confident to use.

NOTE: *Questions and answers in red are examples only. Other responses are possible.*

Prompt Card 1A (Candidate A)

SCHOOL SPORTS DAY

Join us on Friday, 20th July at Wilson Street Sports Ground. The fun starts at 11 am.

Parking: Car park in front of Sports Ground

Tickets: Adults   £1.00
Students   Free

Prompt Card 1B (Candidate B)

SCHOOL SPORTS DAY

♦ When?
B: When is the School Sports Day?
A: (It's on) Friday, 20th July.

♦ Where?
B: Where is the School Sports Day?
A: (It's at) Wilson Street Sports Ground.

♦ Parking?
B: Where can I park my car?
A: In front of the sports ground.

♦ Start?
B: What time does it start?
A: (It starts at) 11 am.

♦ Tickets?
B: How much are the tickets?
A: £1 for adults. Students are free.

Prompt Card 2A (Candidate B)

HI-TECH EXHIBITION

Hundreds of exhibits!
Computers – mobile phones –
MP3 players ... and much, much more

Exhibition Centre, Manshaw Road
14th – 21st August
10 am – 8 pm
Monday to Saturday

Tickets: Free

See local newspapers
for a list of special events.

Prompt Card 2B (Candidate A)

HI-TECH EXHIBITION

♦ Where?
A: Where is the exhibition?
B: (It's at) the Exhibition Centre in Manshaw Road.

♦ When?
A: When is the exhibition?
B: (It's from) 14th - 21st August

♦ Times?
A: What are the times?
B: 10 am - 8 pm.

♦ Tickets?
A: How much are the tickets?
B: They are free.

♦ Special events?
A: Are there any special events?
B: Yes, there are. (You can see them in the newspaper.)

A

SIMILAR BUT DIFFERENT – Use the words in the box to fill in the gaps in each group.

1 | **just** | **exactly**

a The 8 o'clock train has ....just............ arrived. It's an hour late.

b The train arrived on time, at ....exactly......... 8 o'clock.

2 | **hardly** | **hard**

a There is ....hardly.......... any milk in the fridge. We need to buy some more.

b Henry is tired. He's been studying ....hard............ for his exams.

3 | **before** | **ago**

a I have to finish my homework ....before.......... I can watch TV.

b I finished my homework ten minutes ....ago............ . Now I am watching TV.

4 | **live** | **stay**

a Wendy and Jim ....live............ in a flat in Manchester.

b We always ....stay........... at luxury hotels when we go on holiday.

5 | **to** | **too** | **two**

a It's ....too............ cold ....to............. swim in winter.

b Mrs Jones has ....two............ children, and Mrs Allen does, ...too............ .

c I am thinking of inviting all my classmates ....to.............. my birthday party.

B

SPELLING – Circle the spelling mistake in each sentence. Then rewrite the word correctly on the right.

1 They always have their (brekfast) at 8 o'clock. ....breakfast.......................

2 Jenny is not (feelling) well today. ....feeling.......................

3 Sam is (makeing) something to eat at the moment. ....making.......................

4 Steven works in a (langauge) school. ....language.......................

5 (Acommodation) is available in the Halls of Residence. ....Accommodation.......................

6 I need a break. I've been (studing) all day. ....studying.......................

7 We have (hundrends) of CDs. ....hundreds.......................

8 The students are (siting) at their desks now. ....sitting.......................

C

QUESTION WORDS – Use the words in the box to complete the gaps in question 1-6. Then match each question to the appropriate answer. The first one has been done as an example.

| **how** | **what** | **when** | **where** | **who** | **why** |

1 ....What................ is the capital of England? **A** On 26th July.

2 ....Where............... is the station? **B** £45.

3 ....Who............... is your best friend? **C** Mary.

4 ....Why.............. were you late for the lesson? **D** London.

5 ....When............ does the term end? **E** It's on Princess Street.

6 ....How............. much is this pair of jeans? **F** Because I missed the bus.

D   DIALOGUE BUILDING – Look at each response. Write the question.

1   **A:**   When's your birthday?
     B: My birthday is next month.

2   **A:**   Where is the bank?
     B: The bank? It's on Bridge Street.

3   **A:**   What's your favourite colour?
     B: My favourite colour is red.

4   **A:**   How much did the tickets cost?
     B: The tickets? They cost £5 each.

5   **A:**   Who's coming to the party?
     B: All my friends are coming. It'll be a great party!

6   **A:**   How many eggs have we got?
     B: We've got three eggs.

7   **A:**   How long / How many years is the course?
     B: It's a three-year course.

8   **A:**   Why is Mum angry?
     B: Mum? She's angry because my room is messy.

E   WRITING

1   Read the letter from George. Write the three questions you must answer on the right.

I'm really looking forward to spending my holidays with you and your family. Please tell me what the weather will be like, how far it is to the nearest beach and whether it will be hot enough to go swimming.
George

GEORGE'S QUESTIONS

1   What will the weather be like?

2   How far is it to the nearest beach?

3   Will it be hot enough to go swimming?

2   Look at three students' answers to the letter. Then answer the questions by putting A, B or C in the space.

A
Dear George
It will be hot. The nearest beach is only 500 Meters away, if it is sunny we can swim
Leanne

B
Dear George,
I really like hot whether, I hate the winter when it rains a lot. Their are lots of nice beaches in my country. We will be able to go swiming every day.

C
Dear George,
The weather will be sunny. There are lots of nice beaches. The best one is only a short walk from my home. It will be hot enough to go swimming every day.
Sue

Which letter ...

does not answer all the questions?   ...B...

is too short?   ...A...

forgets to use a closing?   ...B...

has serious punctuation errors?   ...A...

has several spelling mistakes?   ...B...

would get the highest mark?   ...C...

Part 1

Questions 1 – 5

Which notice (**A – H**) says this (**1 – 5**)?

For questions **1 – 5**, mark the correct letter **A – H** on your answer sheet.

Example:

0 ...C... We can tell you how to get to places.

Answer:

0	A	B	C	D	E	F	G	H

---

1 ...D... Do not put in washing machine.

A | **NO RIGHT TURN**

2 ...A... Cars can only go left here.

B | CLOSED FOR REPAIRS – BACK ON MONDAY.

3 ...G... Stand here until someone shows you to your table.

C | **TRAVEL CENTRE**

4 ...B... We will reopen after the weekend.

D | Hand wash only

5 ...E... You cannot buy tickets here at the weekend.

E | **BOX OFFICE** Open 9 am – 9 pm Monday – Friday

Tip

Sometimes several signs may have the same word or phrase as one of the sentences. To work out the answer, read each sign carefully, underline the key words and compare them to the key words in the sentence on the left.

TRY IT! - Look at Part 1 again. Answer the questions.

Sentence 1 contains the word 'washing'.

1 Which 2 signs contain the word 'wash'? ...D, H...

2 Which refers to washing one's hands? ...H...

3 Which refers to washing an item of clothing by hand? ...D...

4 Which best relates to sentence 1? ...D...

F | *SPECIAL OFFER* PRE-SHOW – £12.50

G | Please wait for hostess to seat you

H | Employees must wash hands.

Part 2

Questions 6 – 10

Read the sentences about working.
Choose the best word (**A**, **B** or **C**) for each space.

For questions **6 – 10**, mark **A**, **B** or **C** on your answer sheet.

Example:

0   Alan ………. his new job last week.

    A applied   **B** went   **(C)** started   *Answer:*

---

6   Sally ………. the company two years ago.

    A came   **B** arrived   **(C)** joined

7   It is important to make a good impression when you ………. for an interview.

    (A) go   **B** attend   **C** give

8   Our last boss was very nice, but the ………. one is really unfriendly.

    A first   **B** next   **(C)** new

9   Jeff was unemployed for a long time before he finally ………. a job.

    A looked   **(B)** found   **C** did

10   Martha turned up late for ………. again today.

    (A) work   **B** job   **C** business

Tip

Always check for a preposition before or after the gap. If there is a preposition, make sure the word you choose can be used with it. If there is no preposition, make sure the word you choose can be used without a preposition

TRY IT! - Circle any prepositions you find after the gaps. Then underline the answers.

1	Alan …………….(for)a new job last week.	applied	started
	Alan ……………. his new job last week.	applied	started
2	Rita …………….(to)the office late.	got	arrived
	Rita …………….(at)the office late.	got	arrived
3	Have you ……………. a job yet?	looked	found
	Have you …………….(for)a job yet?	looked	found

Part 3

Questions 11 – 15

Complete the five conversations.

For questions **11 – 15**, mark **A, B** or **C** on your answer sheet.

Example:

0   What do you do in your free time?

A   I listen to music.

B   The cinema.

C   At weekends.

Answer: 0   A B C

---

11   A kilo of biscuits, please.

A   That's very heavy, isn't it?
(B)   Plain or chocolate?
C   Not for me, thanks.

12   Can I book a table, please?

(A)   Certainly, sir.
B   No, thank you.
C   Sorry, we're sold out.

13   Shall we go to the beach this afternoon?

A   I'll come, too.
(B)   Brilliant idea!
C   I doubt it.

14   Would you like me to drive?

A   No, I don't.
B   Yes, I'd like to.
(C)   Thanks. I'd appreciate it.

15   What time are you meeting Joan?

(A)   At 6 o'clock.
B   I hope she's not late.
C   No, it's too early.

Tip

Always try to determine the function (or purpose) of a question or statement before you try to find the answer.

TRY IT! – Look at questions 11 – 15 again, and answer these questions.

Which dialogue begins with:

a question about time? ......15......   a polite request? ......11......   a polite offer? ......14......
a suggestion? ......13......   a *yes/no* question? ......12......

Questions 16 – 20

Complete the conversation.
What does the hotel receptionist say to Sandy?
For questions **16 – 20**, mark the correct letter **A – H** on your answer sheet.

Example:

Receptionist:	*Grange Hotel. Can I help you?*		
Sandy:	**0** ....*F*....	*Answer:*	**0** A B C D E F G H

Receptionist:	Certainly. What kind of room would you like to book?	**A**	I'm not sure. Either by bus or by train.
Sandy:	**16** ....E....	**B**	Two nights, Friday and Saturday.
Receptionist:	I'm sorry, but we don't have any free. This is our busiest time of year, and those rooms go very quickly.	**C**	Yes, I suppose that's true. Do you have *any* singles free?
Sandy:	**17** ....C....	**D**	What kind of rooms do you have left?
Receptionist:	Yes, we have a few left. How long will you be staying?	**E**	Do you have any single rooms with a sea view?
Sandy:	**18** ....B....		
Receptionist:	Can I have your name, please?	**F**	Yes, I'd like to book a room from Friday, the 12th of July.
Sandy:	**19** ....G....		
Receptionist:	What time will you be arriving?	**G**	Jones, Sandy Jones.
Sandy:	**20** ....H....		
Receptionist:	OK! Thank you for calling.	**H**	About 7 o'clock.

Tip

- As you begin filling in the gaps, it helps to underline key words and then look for options that contain the same word or a similar word (e.g., a synonym or a pronoun).
- You can often narrow down the options by looking at the kind of question the speaker asks: e.g., answers to *yes/no* questions begin with *Yes, No, Certainly* or similar language.
- Before you select an option, make sure that it also fits with what comes *after* the gap.

TRY IT! - Look at the question before item 16, and answer these questions.

1   Which 3 options contain the word room or rooms? - ....D, E, F....
2   Is the Receptionist's question a *yes/no* or information question? ....an information question....
3   Which option can you rule out immediately? ....F (it answers a *yes/no* question - and it's also the example!)....
4   Look at the Receptionist's answer (before item 17). Notice the phrase: "we don't have any free."
    Which option is the best answer to item 16? ....E.... Why? ....Because Sandy asks for a specific type of room, which the Receptionist refers to before item 17.

Part 4

Questions 21 – 27

Read the article about rain and then answer the questions.

For questions **21 – 27**, mark **A, B** or **C** on your answer sheet.

It's Raining *What*?

If you happen to be in England when it's raining hard, you will probably hear someone say, 'It's raining cats and dogs.' Nobody knows how this expression started and, as far as we know, it has never happened. But if cats and dogs don't rain down on us, other things do!

In August 2004, in Knighton, England, John Dean was putting his shopping in his car when it started to rain. Suddenly, he felt something hit him on the head. When he turned, he saw lots of small fish on the ground. Imagine his surprise when he realised they were coming down with the rain.

Two years earlier, the people of Korona in northern Greece had reported another fish shower, and there have been others outside Europe: in India, Singapore, and even the USA.

Some people blame it on global warming or pollution, but scientists disagree. People have reported fish showers since ancient times. Pliny the Elder, a Roman philosopher, was the first to report one in the 1st century A.D.

So, what's the explanation? Meteorologists say that in bad weather strong winds can pick up small objects and carry them long distances. When there's a storm, these objects fall with the rain. And fish are not the only things that rain down. There have been showers of many things, including frogs, tomatoes, coal, and even jellyfish!

Example:

0	According to the passage, which of the following have fallen from the sky?	A	dogs
		B	cats
		Ⓒ	fish

Answer: 0 | A | B | C |

---

21 When it started raining, John Dean was

A   in a supermarket.
Ⓑ   outside his car.
C   inside his car.

22 John Dean was surprised when he

A   felt the raindrops on his head.
B   dropped some fish on the ground.
Ⓒ   realised where the fish came from.

23 What is true about fish showers?

Ⓐ   They have happened around the world.
B   They last for hundreds of years.
C   They have only happened in Europe.

24 According to the writer, when was the first written report of a fish shower?

A   August 2004
B   December 2002
Ⓒ   1st century A.D.

25 Pliny the Elder was

A   an old man.
Ⓑ   a philosopher.
C   a reporter.

26 Fish showers are caused by

A   pollution.
B   global warming.
Ⓒ   bad weather.

27 Which group of experts have explained what causes fish showers?

A   philosophers
Ⓑ   meteorologists
C   reporters

Tip

- Before you try the questions, always read through the text quickly. This helps you get a feel for what the story or article is about, and also gets you familiar with where information is located.
- Once you have read through the text, you are ready to begin. Work through the questions one at a time. Read each question, then go through the text to find the answer. It helps to underline key words in both the question and text.
- **Remember:** the questions always follow the order of the text.

Part 5

Questions 28 – 35

Read the article about brain food.
Choose the best word (**A, B,** or **C**) for each space.

For questions **28 – 35**, mark **A, B** or **C** on your answer sheet.

Brain Food

For the past **(0)** .... years in England,
supermarkets have been selling more healthy foods
in late April and early May. Last year sales of fish in
England **(28)** .... by over 30%, while in Ireland,
sales of blueberries, which some people believe can help your memory, increased by **(29)** ....
incredible 70%.

At first, supermarket managers were puzzled by **(30)** .... increases, **(31)** .... they
soon realised that school and university exams are in late April and early May. Students
appear to be eating healthy foods at this time because they hope that these foods will help
them **(32)** .... better in their exams.

But can you really eat your way to a better grade? Not according to Joyce Stirling, a nutrition
expert: 'There's very little scientific evidence that any one food is good **(33)** .... your
brain. Eating a variety of foods is important for our health. Perhaps the **(34)** .... advice for
anyone taking exams is: get a good night's sleep the night before; eat a light healthy meal
before the exam; and **(35)** .... away from junk food – at least until your exams are over.'

Example:

0	(A) few	**B** little	**C** lot	*Answer:*

0	A	B	C

---

28   **A** raised   (B) rose   **C** risen

29   (A) an   **B** a   **C** the

30   **A** this   **B** that   (C) these

31   (A) but   **B** because   **C** if

32   (A) do   **B** make   **C** feel

33   **A** at   (B) for   **C** by

34   **A** good   **B** better   (C) best

35   **A** go   **B** throw   (C) stay

Think about it!

Questions with Verbs

- **Scenario 1 (question 28)**   raised   rose   risen

When the options are closely related verb forms, it's clear you're being tested on tense and/or commonly confused verbs (e.g., *lie/lay* or *rise/raise*). Look at the paragraph that the gap falls in. What tense(s) are the other sentences in? What time expressions do you have to work with?

- **Scenario 2 (question 32)**   do   make   feel

Check before and after the gap. There are no prepositions or adverbs nearby, so you can be fairly certain that the question is probably testing a common idiom or word combination. Read the sentences before and after the gap. Try putting in each verb in the gap, and reread the sentence. Which word makes the most sense in context?

- **Scenario 3 (question 35)**   go   throw   stay

Check before and after the gap. You will see the words 'away from', which is a clear sign that the question is testing your knowledge of common phrasal verbs. Read the nearby sentences. Try putting each verb in the gap, and reread the sentence. Which word makes the most sense in context?

Part 6

Questions 36 – 40

Read the descriptions of some things you things you can find in a theatre.
What is the word for each one?

The first letter is already there. There is one space for each other letter in the word.

For questions **36 – 40**, write the words on your answer sheet.

Example:

0   This tells you more about what you are going to see.   p r o g r a m m e

                                                    Answer: | **0** | *programme* |

36   This is where you stand if you are in a play or a show.   s t a g e

37   This is a group of people who watch a play.   a u d i e n c e

38   You need one of these to get into the theatre.   t i c k e t

39   You go through here when you leave the theatre.   e x i t

40   These are the clothes that the actors wear.   c o s t u m e s

---

Tip

British vs. American Spelling

Although American spelling is acceptable in other parts of the exam, Part 6 tests standard British spelling. If you are sure you know a word, but find yourself with too many or too few letters to fill in the gaps, it may be that you're trying to use American spelling. Item (0) is a good example of where things can go wrong. If you had used the American spelling (*program*), your answer would be two letters short.

If you've been preparing for both British and American exams, keep this in mind on the day of the exam! Here is a list of words that you might want to watch out for. In each case, the British spelling comes first.

colour - color	*centre - center*	*jewellery - jewelry*	*analyse - analyze*
favour - favor	*metre - meter*	*skilful - skillful*	*criticise - criticize*
honour - honor	*theatre - theater*	*travelling - traveling*	*memorise - memorize*

Part 7

Questions 41 – 50

Complete these two notes.
Write ONE word for each space.

For questions **41 – 50**, write the words on your answer sheet.

Example: | **0** | *here* |

Dear Julie,

We are having a great time (0) .....*here*..... in Portugal. The weather is great. It's hot
(41) ......and..... sunny.

The hotel is (42) ......not...... very big, but it's very comfortable. (43) .....There... is a great view
of the beach from our balcony. We have breakfast (44) ......on...... the balcony every day.

I'd like (45) ....to....... stay in Portugal forever!

Love,

Susan

Dear Susan,

Thanks (46) ......for...... your card. It was really great to (47) ....hear.... from you. I'm glad you're
(48) ..having... a good time.

Enjoy the rest (49) ......of....... your holiday. See you (50) ....when.... you get back.

Julie

Tip
Part 7
Remember: You may write only one word in the gap.

Tip
Part 8
Remember: This is a note-taking exercise. Write words and phrases for answers, not whole sentences.

Part 8

Questions 51 – 55

Read the application letter.
Fill in the information on the Applicant Information Form.

For questions **51 – 55**, write the information on your answer sheet.

---

11 Castle Drive

Harrogate

Yorkshire

20 May

Dear Sir/Madam,

I saw your ad in the local paper and I'm writing to say that I'm interested in a summer position with Manway Computer Store. My name is Gary Hughes. I was born in Australia, and I lived in New Zealand for two years before I came to England.

I am 19 years old, and I am studying economics at university. My last exam is on Friday, 20th June. I will be able to work every day from Monday, the 23rd, until my course starts again on 6th October.

Last year I worked in the box office at the Odeon Cinema, but I would really like to work in a computer shop now.

Yours faithfully,
Gary Hughes

MANWAY COMPUTER STORE
Applicant Information Form

Name:		*Gary Hughes*
Address:	**51**	11 Castle Drive, Harrogate, Yorkshire
Age:	**52**	19/nineteen (years old)
Nationality:	**53**	Australian
Dates available:	**54**	(from) (Monday) 23rd June – 6th October
Experience:	**55**	(box office at) Odeon Cinema

Part 9

Question 56

Read this e-mail from Kim.

Hello!

Thanks for inviting me to your party. I would love to come.

What time does it start? Can I bring a friend? Would you like me to bring anything?

Kim

Write an e-mail to Kim. Answer the questions.

Write **25 – 35** words.

Write the e-mail on your answer sheet.

Tip

Before you begin, list the points you must write about:

1   What time does the party start?
2   Can she bring a friend?
3   Would I like her to bring anything to the party?

Use this list to check your answer:

Have you ...

* told Kim you're glad she's coming?
* written about all 3 points?
* used a closing phrase such as 'Regards' or 'Best wishes'?
* signed your name?
* proofread for grammar, spelling and punctuation?
* checked your word count?

QUESTION 56: MODEL ANSWER

Dear Kim,

I'm glad you're coming. The party starts at 8 pm. Yes, of course you can bring a friend. Could you bring some of your disco CDs with you?

See you soon.

Karen

34 words

Part 1

Questions 1 – 5

You will hear five short conversations.
You will hear each conversation twice.
There is one question for each conversation.
For questions **1 – 5**, put a tick (✔) under the right answer.

Example:

0   How many students are there in the language class?

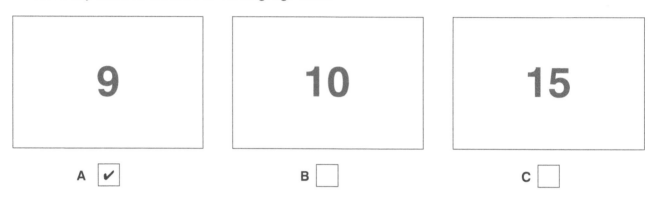

A ✔   B ☐   C ☐

---

1   Where is the hotel?

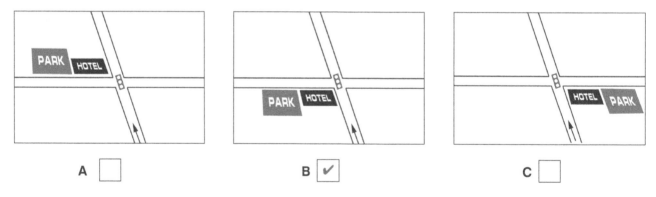

A ☐   B ✔   C ☐

2   Where will Karen and Jim go swimming at the weekend?

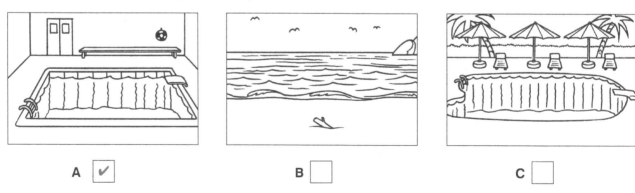

A ✔   B ☐   C ☐

3 How much did the man's meal cost?

£22   £62   £20

A ✔   B ☐   C ☐

4 Where did David buy his trainers?

SPORTS GEAR

A ☐   B ✔   C ☐

5 What time does the circus start on Saturdays?

7 pm   3 pm   8 pm

A ☐   B ☐   C ✔

Tip

Expect Some Indirect References in Questions with Numbers

The speakers in Part 1 will almost always say something about all three pictures. Let's say the question is about 'how many people' and the pictures are a series of numbers. Usually the speakers will mention each number. Sometimes, however, they might refer to one of the numbers in a more indirect way.

A typical example of this is question (0). When we listen, we hear the woman say '10' and '15', but she doesn't say '9' ... or at least not directly. What she does say is: 'There were 10, but 1 of them left'. This is an indirect way of saying that there are now '9' people in her class.

Part 2

Questions 6 – 10

Listen to Christine talking about her holiday.
Where did she spend each day?

For questions **6 – 10**, write a letter (**A – H**) next to each day of the week.
You will hear the conversation twice.

Example:

0	Monday	C

Days of the week

6	Tuesday	D
7	Wednesday	B
8	Thursday	F
9	Friday	E
10	Saturday	A

Activities

A	coffee bar
B	beach
C	Roman villa
D	theme park
E	street market
F	carpet factory
G	museum
H	art gallery

Tip

You hear 'Monday', 'Tuesday', 'Wednesday', 'Friday'. What happened to 'Thursday'?

- When you listen to the dialogue in Part 2, expect to hear the speakers refer to most but not all of the key words in the left-hand column. It's not unusual for one or two of the key words to be referred to in a more indirect way.

  For example, in this exercise the woman does not say 'Thursday'. Instead, after she has told the man what she did on Wednesday, she says 'The next day ... .'

- If you don't hear one or more of the items the first time you listen, listen carefully for a more indirect reference the second time you listen.

Part 3

Questions 11 – 15

Listen to a conversation in a ticket office.

For questions **11 – 15**, tick (✔) **A, B** or **C**.
You will hear the conversation twice.

Example:

0	The man wants tickets for	A	an international theatre festival.	✔
		B	an international film festival.	
		C	an international book fair.	

11	The man can only come to	A	the Greek play.	
		B	the French play.	✔
		C	the Italian play.	

12	There are afternoon performances on	A	Wednesdays.	✔
		B	Saturdays.	
		C	Sundays.	

13	The special performance is at	A	7.30 pm.	
		B	7 pm.	
		C	10 am.	✔

14	The man wants to book tickets for the performance in the	A	morning.	
		B	afternoon.	✔
		C	evening.	

15	Student tickets cost	A	£6.50.	
		B	£8.00.	
		C	£5.00.	✔

Tip

At the start of Part 3, you have 20 seconds to read the questions and options. Use this time to look for clues that will tell you what to listen for.

• Sometimes the options are identical, except for a final word or phrase. This tells you that you need to listen for the phrase they have in common and then pay special attention to what comes immediately after.
• Sometimes the options are different days, times, or places. Underline the key word or phrase in the question stem, then listen carefully for it and the information that follows it.

TRY IT! - Answer the questions.

1 Look at question 0. What two words can you expect to hear right before the answer? an international

2 Look at questions 12, 13, and 15. What key words/phrases must you listen for?
  12 .....afternoon performance.....   13 .....special performance.....   15 .....student tickets.....

Part 4

Questions 16 – 20

You will hear a woman asking for information about a computer.

Listen and complete questions **16 – 20**.
You will hear the conversation twice.

COMPUTER FOR SALE

Type:		Laptop
Colour:	**16**	black and ....silver.........
Memory:	**17**	.........40 / forty........ gigabytes
Accessories:	**18**	mouse and ....microphone....
Type of carrying case:	**19**	black leather ....
Price:	**20**	£ ......425.........

Tip

Numbers: It's as Easy as 1 – 2 – 3

Expect several answers in Parts 4 and 5 to be numbers.

You can either write the number (*1, 2, 3*) or spell out your answers (*one, two, three*). But why not take the easy way out?

Writing the number will save you time . . . and it also means you won't spell anything in a number question incorrectly!

Part 5

Questions 21 – 25

You will hear some information about a special kind of sale at a department store.

Listen and complete questions **21 – 25**.
You will hear the information twice.

Blue Cross Sale

Where:	Sendal's
All items with blue cross:	**21** <u>half / 1/2</u> price
Fashion show times:	**22** <u>11 / eleven</u> am and 3pm
Fashion show days:	**23** daily, except <u>Thursday(s)</u>
Cookery demonstration:	**24** daily, 1-3 pm on the <u>third / 3rd</u> floor
Sale finishes:	**25** end of the <u>month</u>

You now have 8 minutes to write your answers on the answer sheet.

Listening Spotlight 2

Audioscript on page 157.

Questions with numbers appear in all parts of the Listening Paper. Here are some typical examples.

For items 1–3, write the phone numbers you hear.

1 <u>235 7557</u>   3 <u>0800 153 4444</u>

2 <u>0747 126 9005</u>

For items 4–8, underline the numbers you hear.

4	**Years:**	1960	<u>960</u>	1916
5	**Times:**	<u>15.50</u>	15.15	5.50
6	**Miles:**	880	808	<u>818</u>
7	**Prices:**	£19.19	£19.90	£90.19
8	**Dates:**	3rd June	<u>13th June</u>	30th June

Follow-up: Take turns reading the numbers with a partner.

Pronunciation Key

1   two three five – seven double-five seven

2   oh seven four seven – one two six – nine double-oh five

3   oh eight hundred – one five three – double-four double-four.

4   nineteen sixty
    nine sixty
    nineteen sixteen

5   fifteen-fifty; fifteen-fifteen; five-fifty

6   eight hundred and eighty
    eight hundred and eight
    eight hundred and eighteen

7   nineteen pounds nineteen
    nineteen pounds ninety
    ninety pounds nineteen

8   the third of June
    the thirteenth of June
    the thirtieth of June

Part 1 (5 – 6 minutes)

Questions for Both Candidates

What's your name?

What's your surname?

How do you spell that?

Where do you come from?

Do you work or are you a student?

What do you do/study?

Do you like it?

Why?/Why not?

Questions for Candidate A

Do you like playing sports? Why/why not?

Have you been to any foreign countries? Which?/ Which would you like to go to?

What are you going to do after the exam today?

Tell me something about the kind of TV programmes you like.

Questions for Candidate B

Who is your favourite actor?

Do you have any pets?

How often do you go to the cinema?

What did you do last weekend?

Tell me something about the kind of music you like.

Part 2 (3 – 4 minutes)

1   Candidate A, here is some information about a magazine.

Candidate B, you don't know anything about the magazine, so ask A some questions about it. Now B, ask A your questions about the magazine and A, you answer them.

[Candidate A looks at Prompt Card 1A on next page]
[Candidate B looks at Prompt Card 1B on next page]

2   Candidate B, here is some information about a competition.

Candidate A, you don't know anything about the competition, so ask B some questions about it. Now A, ask B your questions about the competition and B, you answer them.

[Candidate B looks at Prompt Card 2A on next page]
[Candidate A looks at Prompt Card 2B on next page]

Frequently Asked Questions: Speaking (Part 2)

- **What should I do if my partner doesn't seem to understand my question?**
  Be prepared to repeat the question. If he or she still doesn't understand, try to rephrase the question using slightly different words. For example:

      A: Who is the magazine for?
      B: Sorry, I didn't understand you.
      A: Who reads the magazine? What kind of people?

- **What should I do if my partner's answer doesn't seem logical or correct?**
  Don't worry. Just say 'thank you' and move on to your next question.
  Remember: *If your partner doesn't answer one or more questions correctly, this will not affect your mark.*

NOTE: *Questions and answers in red are examples only. Other responses are possible.*

Prompt Card 1A (Candidate A)

NOW ON SALE!
**The monthly magazine for people
who love mysteries . . .**

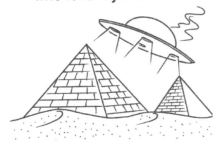

MYSTERIES
In this month's issue:
Special Loch Ness Monster Investigation
FREE CD-ROM INSIDE:
'100 Unexplained Mysteries'
£2.50

Prompt Card 1B (Candidate B)

♦ Name/magazine?
  B: What's the name of the magazine?
  A: (It's called) Mysteries.

♦ Weekly/monthly?
  B: Is it (a) weekly or monthly (magazine)?
  A: (It's a) monthly (magazine).

♦ Who for?
  B: Who is it for?
  A: (It's for) people who love mysteries.

♦ Free gifts?
  B: Are there any free gifts?
  A: Yes, there's a free CD-ROM inside
     (called '100 Unexplained Mysteries').

♦ Cost?
  B: How much does it cost? / What does
     it cost?
  A: (It costs) £2.50 (two pounds fifty).

Prompt Card 2A (Candidate B)

Short Story Competition
FANTASTIC PRIZE:

**Brand new
laptop**

Are you aged between 15 and 18?

Do you like writing stories?

Why not enter our short story competition?

To enter, simply write a short story
(300 – 500 words).

Please send entries before 28th February.

Prompt Card 2B (Candidate A)

Competition

♦ Type / competition?
  A: What type of competition is it?
  B: (It's) a short story competition.

♦ What / prize?
  A: What is the prize?
  B: A (brand new) laptop.

♦ What / age?
  A: What age do I have to be (to enter
     the competition)?
  B: (You have to be) between 15 and 18.

♦ How many / words?
  A: How many words do I have to write?
  B: (You have to write) between 300 and
     500 words.

♦ When / send?
  A: When do I have to send my story/entry?
  B: (You have to send it) before 28th February.

A **SIMILAR BUT DIFFERENT** – Use the words in the box to fill in the gaps in each group.

1 **a few** **a little**

  a The test was really easy, but I think I've made a ....few........... mistakes.

  b Can I have a ....little......... more sugar in my tea, please?

2 **employee** **employer**

  a I work for Smith and Sons. They're one of the biggest .....employers.... in the area.

  b Smith and Sons have over 2,000 ....employees.... .

3 **their** **there**

  a Students are always complaining about ....their......... homework.

  b A new music shop has opened in the shopping centre. You can buy all the new releases ....there......... .

4 **take** **give**

  a I have to ....take......... my English exam next week.

  b The teacher is going to ....give......... us our results this week.

5 **if** **when**

  a Kate will go to university ....if............ she gets good marks in her exams.

  b Harry will go to university ....when....... he gets back from Spain. He's coming home in early September.

B **PREPOSITION PRACTICE** – Use the words in the box to fill in the gaps in the sentences.

in **at** **from** **to**

1 Bill is very interested ....in.......... learning ancient Greek.

2 The maths exam is ....on.......... Tuesday morning.

3 The next performance starts ....at.......... 7 pm.

4 I haven't heard ....from......... Paula since last month.

5 According ....to........... Mark, the party's been cancelled.

6 Gerry has lived ....in.......... Liverpool all his life.

7 Who are you inviting ....to........... your party?

8 I hope that dog stays away ....from......... me. It looks really dangerous.

C **QUESTION WORDS** – Make questions for the words in bold. The first one has been done as an example.

0 John had a **hamburger** for dinner.   What did John have for dinner?

1 Warren was visiting **his parents** yesterday.   Who was Warren visiting yesterday?

2 Sarah goes to the cinema **every Friday**.   How often (When) does Sarah go to the cinema?

3 Dennis has been living in York **for 10 years**.   How long has Dennis been living in York?

4 Eric is going to **Malta** next week.   Where is Eric going next week?

5 Mark is studying **because he has a test**.   Why is Mark studying?

6 The meal cost **£35**.   How much/What did the meal cost?

D **DIALOGUE BUILDING** – Match each question to the appropriate answer. The first one has been done as an example.

0	Are you glad you changed jobs?	**A**	Yes, he did, but he hasn't started yet.
1	Did Mike enjoy his trip to Spain?	**B**	Yes, I am. My new boss is very nice.
2	Who went to Spain for a week last year?	**C**	To the post office. He needs to post a letter.
3	Did Andrew get the job he applied for?	**D**	Yes, he did. In fact, he loved it.
4	How long will they be away?	**E**	Sally did, and she had a great time.
5	Where's Gary going?	**F**	Gary is. He needs to buy some stamps.
6	Who's going to the post office?	**G**	About a week, but it might be longer.

Follow-up: Now compare answers with a partner. Discuss any differences you have, and see if you can agree on a common solution. Be ready to explain your answers.

E **WRITING SKILLS: Proofreading for Spelling**

Mary and John are pen friends. In John's last letter, he asked about her plans for the summer. Read Mary's response. It has 9 spelling mistakes. Circle the mistakes, and write the words correctly on the lines provided. The first has been done as an example.

Hint: There are two mistakes per line after the example.

Hi, John,

I hope you had a (grate) time on your (halliday.) I (usuly) go to my mother's (vilage) with my (familly,) but (these) year I'm going (too) Rome with my (cousens) I can't (weight!)

Write soon,

Mary

great	
holiday	usually
village	family
this	to
cousins	wait

Part 1

Questions 1 – 5

Which notice (**A – H**) says this (**1 – 5**)?

For questions **1 – 5**, mark the correct letter **A – H** on your answer sheet.

Example:

0 ....F.... You cannot buy tickets here.   *Answer:*

0	A	B	C	D	E	F	G	H

---

1 ....D.... You can buy things more cheaply here.

2 ....B.... You cannot use your mobile phone here.

3 ....E.... You cannot eat here.

4 ....C.... You can make a phone call here.

5 ....G.... You should keep this in the fridge.

A
> **EMPLOYEE SNACK BAR**
> Open 9 am – 4.30 pm

B
> **EXAM CENTRE**
> All mobile phones must be switched off.

C
> **PUBLIC TELEPHONES**
> **on 1st floor**

D
> (**BARGAIN BASEMENT**)

E
> **NO FOOD OR DRINK ALLOWED**

F
> **ENQUIRIES ONLY**

G
> Store in a cool place.

H
> Do not re-freeze.

Tip

A sign usually tells you what you can or cannot do. So does a sentence that rephrases the meaning of a sign.

- Always read each sentence carefully and ask yourself: Is it about something you *can* or *should* do or something you *cannot* or *should not* do?

- **Remember:** If a sentence has a negative word, the matching sign will usually have one, too. Watch for words like 'not', 'no', 'never' and 'only'.

Question 0 is an interesting example. The sentence is about something you *cannot* do, but sign F, which matches it, is about something that you can *only* do. What's the connection? Think about it: If a place is for *enquiries only*, then you *cannot buy tickets* there.

TRY IT! - Look at Part 1 again. Answer the questions.

1 Which 3 sentences are about things you cannot do?
...0, 2, 3...............

2 Which 3 signs contain negative words or 'only'?
...E, F, H...............

3 Which sign says you *must* do something, which means you *cannot* do something else? ...B...............
Which sentence does it match? ...2...............

Part 2

Questions 6 – 10

Read the sentences about shopping.
Choose the best word (**A, B** or **C**) for each space.

For questions **6 – 10**, mark **A, B** or **C** on your answer sheet.

Example:

0   Most of the shops in our town are .... Market Street.

(**A**) in   **B** at   **C** to   *Answer:* 0 A B C

---

6   I don't shop at the new supermarket because the prices are .... expensive.

A much   (**B**) too   **C** enough

7   You can get a lot of great bargains in the ....

A discounts   **B** offers   (**C**) sales

8   Have you been to that new clothes shop .... ?

(**A**) yet   **B** still   **C** just

9   Those jeans are really nice, but they aren't .... £150.

A cost   **B** value   (**C**) worth

10   Janet can't come on Saturday morning because she has to .... the shopping.

A make   (**B**) do   **C**   go

Tip

Expect the options to be similar in meaning. Only one of the options will fit both the *structure* and *meaning* of the sentence.

TRY IT! - Underline the correct answers.

1	I haven't talked to Mary	still	<u>yet</u>	just
	I've .... talked to Mary.	still	yet	<u>just</u>
	I .... haven't talked to Mary.	<u>still</u>	yet	just
2	That house is .... £500,00.	cost	valued	<u>worth</u>
	That house .... £500,000.	<u>cost</u>	valued	worth
	That house is .... at £500,000.	cost	<u>valued</u>	worth

Part 3

Questions 11 – 15

Complete the five conversations.

For questions **11 – 15**, mark **A**, **B** or **C** on your answer sheet.

Example:

0

| What do you do in your free time? |

A I listen to music.

B The cinema.

C At weekends.

Answer:

| 0 | A | B | C |

---

11   Would you like a starter with your meal?

    (A)   Yes, please.
    B   I hope so.
    C   I like it very much.

12   When did you get back from France?

    A   For two weeks.
    (B)   Last Sunday.
    C   In two days' time.

13   I'm sorry. We don't have any left.

    A   That's right.
    B   I'd like to buy them.
    (C)   What a pity!

14   Is anyone sitting here?

    (A)   Yes, I'm afraid so.
    B   He's late again.
    C   No, you're not.

15   This is my friend, Mary.

    (A)   Pleased to meet you.
    B   I like her, too.
    C   John is my friend.

Tip

- Before you answer, it helps to think about the situation in each question. Ask yourself questions like:
  Who are the two speakers?   Where are they?   Is the situation formal or informal?
- Remember: The more you understand about the situation, the more likely you are to find the answer.

TRY IT! - Look at questions 11 – 15 again. Underline the answers.

1	Question 11 probably takes place in	a cinema	<u>a restaurant</u>	an office
2	The speakers in question 12 are probably	<u>friends</u>	strangers	a waiter and customer
3	The second speaker in question 13 probably feels	happy	<u>disappointed</u>	angry
4	Question 14 probably takes place in	a cinema	a baker's	a clothing shop
5	The second speaker in question 15 is	agreeing	disagreeing	<u>responding to an introduction</u>

Questions 16 – 20

Complete the conversation.
What does Irene say to Ray?
For questions **16 – 20**, mark the correct letter **A – H** on your answer sheet.

Example:

Ray: When are you coming to visit us?

Irene: **0**   .....*B*.....

Answer: | 0 | A | B | C | D | E | F | G | H |

Ray:	I think I left my jacket at your place. Can you have a look for it, please?	**A**	It's already in my bag. I found it just after you left.
Irene:	**16** .....A.....	**B**	Next weekend. Would you like me to bring anything?
Ray:	Thanks. How long can you stay this time?		
Irene:	**17** .....D.....	**C**	For the last two weeks, I think.
Ray:	What would you like to do when you're here?	**D**	Not long. I have to be back at college on Monday morning.
Irene:	**18** .....E.....		
Ray:	Sounds great. I'll get the details. What about the next day?	**E**	There's an open air concert on Saturday. Could we go to that?
Irene:	**19** .....F.....	**F**	I thought we could have a picnic in the park if the weather's okay.
Ray:	Brilliant! I'll invite Jay and Lena, too.		
Irene:	**20** .....G.....	**G**	Fantastic! I haven't seen either of them since I started college.
Ray:	Great! Just text me when you arrive, and I'll come and meet you.	**H**	Sunday, I think.

Tip

Pronouns like *I, me, my, mine, you, your(s), we, us,* and *our(s)* frequently appear in long dialogues, but other pronouns also play a role. Here are some things to think about:

• When you choose an option with a **pronoun**, make sure it matches a noun in the speech before it.
• Similarly, when you choose an option that includes one or more **nouns**, check the response after the gap to make sure any pronouns there relate back to the nouns in the option.

TRY IT! - Look at the dialogue again and answer the questions.

1   Look at Ray's speech before item 16. What does the pronoun *it* refer back to? ....'my (his) jacket'....
Which option also includes *it*? ......A...... Is this the answer to item 16? .....yes.....

2   The correct answer to item 20 uses a pronoun to refer back to something or someone Ray mentions.
What is the pronoun? .....them..... Who or what does it refer back to? .....Jay and Lena.....

Part 4

Questions 21 – 27

Read the article about a TV series.
Are sentences **21 – 27** 'Right' (**A**) or 'Wrong' (**B**)?
If there is not enough information to answer 'Right' (**A**) or 'Wrong' (**B**), choose 'Doesn't say' (**C**).

For questions **21 – 27**, mark **A, B** or **C** on your answer sheet.

Europe's Longest Running Soap Opera

At 7 pm on 9th December 1960, a new programme about an imaginary place called Weatherfield in the North of England was shown on British TV. The show was called *Florizel Street*, but later its name was changed to *Coronation Street*. It was written by 19-year-old Tony Warren, who based it on his grandmother's neighbourhood in the North West of England.

The programme was about the people who lived in Coronation Street. Warren wrote twelve episodes for the first season. And, in case the series failed, he also wrote a final episode about a builder's plans to knock down the houses on the street and build something new.

To viewers' relief, this episode has never been shown. *Coronation Street* was an instant success. Over 6,000 episodes later, it's still the most popular 'soap' in Britain. *'Corrie'*, as many call it, is now shown five times weekly and about 9 million people watch each episode. There are *Coronation Street* web sites, fan clubs and chat rooms. Books have been written about it and it is even studied on university courses. Over the years Corrie's actors have become famous, and many celebrities have appeared on 'the street', including members of the British royal family.

'Corrie' is not only shown in Britain. You can also watch it in Canada, Australia and Sweden … and really anywhere that satellite television can reach.

Example:

0   Weatherfield is a town in the North of England.

   A Right   **(B)** Wrong   **C** Doesn't say   *Answer:*

0	A	B	C

---

21   People did not like the name *Florizel Street*.

   A Right   **B** Wrong   **(C)** Doesn't say

22   The first episodes of *Coronation Street* were written by a teenager.

   (A) Right   **B** Wrong   **C** Doesn't say

23   Tony Warren still writes all the episodes of *Coronation Street*.

   A Right   **B** Wrong   **(C)** Doesn't say

24   6,000 people watch each episode of *Coronation Street*.

   A Right   **(B)** Wrong   **C** Doesn't say

25   You can find information about *Coronation Street* on the Internet.

   (A) Right   **B** Wrong   **C** Doesn't say

26   Thanks to modern technology, people all over the world can watch *'Corrie'*.

   (A) Right   **B** Wrong   **C** Doesn't say

27   Members of the British royal family appear in every episode of the popular show.

   A Right   **(B)** Wrong   **C** Doesn't say

Tip

The Dangers of 'Word-Spotting'

As you do each question, you'll naturally want to find the key words in the question then read through the passage quickly to find those words. But be careful! Here's an example of what can go wrong:

The example, question (0), says that a place called **Weatherfield** is a **town** in the **North of England**. Now you have to decide whether the statement is 'right' or 'wrong' or 'doesn't say', so you start to read quickly. In the middle of line 2, you see 'Weatherfield' and 'North of England'. 'Hooray!' you say. 'I've got it! The statement is right!' 'Not so fast,' says your teacher. 'You've found the key words, but what about the beginning of the sentence?' You go back and read the whole sentence, and you see your mistake: Weatherfield is an **imaginary town** in the North of England, which means the statement is 'wrong'!

So, don't be a 'word-spotter'. It's OK to read quickly till you find the key words you're looking for. But after that, always read the whole sentence *and* the surrounding sentences before you choose your answer.

Part 5

Questions 28 – 35

Read the article about driving in England.
Choose the best word (**A, B,** or **C**) for each space.

For questions **28 – 35**, mark **A, B** or **C** on your answer sheet.

Why do the English drive on the 'wrong' side of the road?

Visitors to Britain often wonder **(0)** .... the British are the only people who still drive their cars on the left-hand side of the road. Actually, the British are **(28)** .... alone. Over two billion people **(29)** .... over 70 countries still drive on the left.

Some experts believe that in the Middle Ages most people in Europe drove **(30)** .... carts and carriages and rode their horses on the left because it was safer. Staying on the left **(31)** .... it easier for them to use their swords if robbers attacked them from the opposite direction. Recently, when archaeologists **(32)**.......... examining a Roman site in England, they discovered that even in ancient times people travelled on the left.

So when did people in Europe decide to change sides? One suggestion is that during the 1800s Napoleon forced countries to change to the right. The countries **(33)** .... did not take over continued to drive on the left. This **(34)**.......... why half of Europe drove on the right, while the other half drove on the left.

Europe remained fairly equally divided until the 20th century, when **(35)** .... countries changed to the right. The last country to change sides was Sweden on 3rd September 1967. Britain, Eire, Cyprus and Malta continue to drive on the left.

Example:

0   (A) why   B how   C who   *Answer:* | 0 | A | B | C |
                                                                              | | ▬ | ☐ | ☐ |

---

28   **A** never   **B** nothing   (C) not

29   (A) in   **B** at   **C** to

30   **A** there   **B** they   (C) their

31   **A** did   (B) made   **C** was

32   (A) were   **B** was   **C** are

33   (A) he   **B** who   **C** that

34   **A** proves   (B) explains   **C** tells

35   **A** all   **B** any   (C) most

Think about it!

In Test 2 we looked at typical Part 5 verb questions. Here are two more areas that are commonly tested.
- **Words that sound alike (question 30)**   there   they   their
When the options are words that sound alike, you need to slow down and ask yourself what's missing to get the right answer. In question 30 you need a word that completes the phrase: 'most people in Europe drove .... carts and carriages'. You need to ask yourself *whose carts?* ... and that should lead you to the right answer.

- **Quantity words (question 35)**   all   any   most
When faced with choices that are quantity words, you usually have to go back to the text and look carefully at both the structure and meaning of the gapped sentence. We know *any* is used mostly in questions and negative sentences, so that's probably not the answer here. To choose between *all* and *most*, you must go back to the text and consider the overall meaning of the paragraph. Ask yourself, 'Did *all* countries change to the right in the 20th century, or were there a few that didn't?' If you read to the end of the paragraph, the answer is there in black and white!

Part 6

Questions 36 – 40

Read the descriptions of words about TV.
What is the word for each one?

The first letter is already there. There is one space for each other letter in the word.

For questions **36 – 40**, write the words on your answer sheet.

Example:

0   This is a TV show that makes you laugh.   c o m e d y

Answer: | 0 | comedy |

36   I take part in a game show or quiz.   c o n t e s t a n t

37   This is another name for a TV station.   c h a n n e l

38   We watch TV.   v i e w e r s

39   I introduce a TV show.   p r e s e n t e r

40   Television shows are recorded here.   s t u d i o

Tip

In the Tips for Part 6 in Tests 1 and 2 we looked at some of the things you can look at if the word you spell is too long or too short. Here are some other possibilities:

• Sometimes the word you spell may be too short. Did you forget to double one of the letters?

• Sometimes the word you spell may be too long. Did you double a letter when you didn't need to?

TRY IT! - Correct the mistakes in these answers.

1   This is a television advertisement.   c o m e r c i a l   c o m m e r c i a l

2   This control makes the sound louder or softer.   v o l l u m e   v o l u m e

3   This is another word for 'show'.   p r o g r a m e   p r o g r a m m e

Part 7

Questions 41 – 50

Complete these e-mails.
Write ONE word for each space.

For questions **41 – 50**, write the words on your answer sheet.

Example: | **0** | *like*

Dear Maria,

Would you (0) ....*like*...... a pen-friend? I've just read (41) ....*an*........ advert in an English magazine for pen-friends. I want a pen-friend (42) ...*because*... I think (43) ....*it*........ will improve my English.

I (44) .....*hope*..... you are interested (45) ....*in*........ having a pen-friend, too.

Sally

Dear Sally,

What a great idea! I (46) .....*would*.... love to have a pen-friend! Perhaps we could visit (47) ....*our*....... pen-friends, too, or we could invite (48) .....*them*..... to visit us. (49) .....*What*..... do you think? Last summer my cousin Audrey went to visit her Canadian pen-friend Janet, (50) ....*whose*.... family has a summer home in Nova Scotia. She had a fantastic time, and Janet is coming here this summer.

Maria

Tip

Watch Your Possessives

Question 47 tests a grammar point that many KET candidates have problems with. Students often confuse personal pronouns (*I/me, he/him, she/her, it/it, we/us, you/you, they/them*), possessive adjectives (*my, your, his, her, its, our, their*) and possessive pronouns (*mine, yours, his, hers, ours, theirs*).

Remember: Except for *its*, a possessive form that comes before a noun never ends in *-s*.

TRY IT! - Underline the correct form(s) in each sentence.

1 '*Who's* / *Whose* keys are on the table'?   'They're my / *mine*.'

2 Those aren't *your* / *yours* shoes. They're Dan's. *Your* / *Yours* are under the bed.

3 Don't grab the cat by *it's* / *its* tail. *It's* / *Its* cruel to do that!

4 *There* / *Their* is a lovely house for sale on the corner. It can be *their* / *theirs* if they make a good offer!

Part 8

Questions 51 – 55

Read the notice and Helen's letter to Wendy.
Complete Wendy's notes.

For questions **51 – 55**, write the information on your answer sheet.

Important Notice

All flights to Spain on Monday,
10th May, have been cancelled.

Next available flights:
Tuesday, 11th May, 6 am
Wednesday, 12th May, 3 pm

Hi, Wendy,

Can you call Jane, please, and tell her our flight has been cancelled?

There is a flight the next day early in the morning, but it doesn't give us much time to get to the airport, so I've booked the afternoon flight on Wednesday.

Mum can't drive us to the airport because Dad needs the car for work. Can you ask Jane to call Castle Cab Company and arrange a taxi for around 11 am? That will get us to the airport by 12 o'clock.

Thanks,

Helen

WENDY'S NOTES

Flight on 10th May:		*cancelled*
New flight date:	**51**	12th May
Time:	**52**	3 pm / three pm
Travel to airport:	**53**	by ....taxi........
Name of taxi company:	**54**	Castle Cab Company
Arrive at airport:	**55**	12 o'clock

Part 9

Question 56

Read this note from your English friend, Carl.

Hi, there!

We don't have any classes tomorrow evening so let's go to the cinema.

There is a comedy on at the Odeon. It's on at 5.30 and 8.30 pm. Let me know which time is best for you, and where and when you want me to meet you.

Carl

Write Carl a note. Answer the questions.

Write **25 – 35** words.

Write the note on your answer sheet.

Tip

Before you begin, list the points you must write about:

1 best time
2 where to meet
3 what time to meet

Use this list to check your answer:

Have you ...

• told your friend you like his idea and why?

• written about all 3 points?

• used a closing phrase such as 'Regards' or 'Best wishes'?

• signed your name?

• proofread for grammar, spelling and punctuation?

• checked your word count?

QUESTION 56: MODEL ANSWER

Dear Carl,

The cinema sounds great. I haven't seen a comedy for ages! The best time for me is 5.30. Meet me at the bus station on King Street at 5.15.

See you soon.
[Name]

35 words

Part 1

Questions 1 – 5

You will hear five short conversations.
You will hear each conversation twice.
There is one question for each conversation.
For questions **1 – 5**, put a tick (✔) under the right answer.

Example:

0   How many students are there in the language class?

9	**10**	**15**
A ✔	B ☐	C ☐

---

1   What will the weather be like at the weekend?

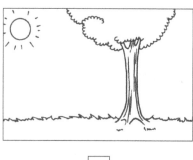  

A ✔   B ☐   C ☐

2   Where do the man's parents live?

London	**Brighton**	**Madrid**
A ☐	B ✔	C ☐

3 Which phone will the woman buy?

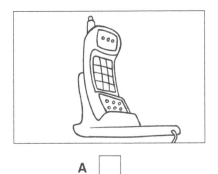 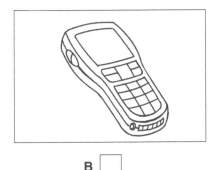 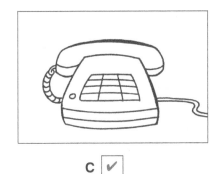

A ☐   B ☐   C ✔

4 How will the man spend the evening?

A ☐   B ☐   C ✔

5 How long will it take them to drive to the airport?

| 1 hour | 1½ hours | 40 minutes |

A ✔   B ☐   C ☐

Tip

Past, Present or Future

Some questions in this part test your ability to understand whether the speakers are talking about the past, present or future. For this reason, it's important to notice the tense used in the question. Then pay careful attention to the tense the speakers use when they talk about each option.

Question 2 is a good example. Both the narrator and the woman ask where the man's parents are living now. If you listen carefully, you'll notice that the man uses the Past Simple to talk about two of the options. He then switches to the Present Continuous when he talks about where his parents are living now.

Part 2

Questions 6 – 10

Listen to Gerry and Penny planning a family trip to London.
What place do they choose for each person to visit?

For questions **6 – 10**, write a letter (**A – H**) next to each person.
You will hear the conversation twice.

Example:

0	Sally	H

6	Billy	B		**A**	West End theatre
7	Dad	F		**B**	Zoo
8	Mum	A		**C**	Shops in Oxford Street
9	Penny	C		**D**	Madame Tussauds
10	Gerry	D		**E**	Thames Cruise
				F	Covent Garden
				G	Houses of Parliament
				H	London Eye

Tip

Use the Second Listening Wisely

Don't panic if you don't answer all the questions on the first listening. Answer as many questions as you can the first time you hear the recording. Then use the second listening to check the questions you answered and fill in anything you missed the first time.

If you still have unanswered questions after the second listening, guess! You don't lose marks for wrong answers ... and you have a good chance of getting a question right if you've narrowed down the choices.

Part 3

Questions 11 – 15

Listen to Hillary asking for information about a gym.

For questions **11 – 15**, tick (✔) **A, B** or **C**.
You will hear the conversation twice.

Example:

0	The first Shapers Gym was in	A	London.	☐
		B	Manchester.	✔
		C	Aberdeen.	☐

11	Shapers now has	A	a million customers.	☐
		B	155 gyms in the UK.	✔
		C	a thousand gyms.	☐

12	The Shapers Gym nearest to Hillary is	A	in a hotel.	☐
		B	in the city centre.	☐
		C	in a shopping centre.	✔

13	At Shapers you can	A	do aerobics.	☐
		B	use special equipment.	✔
		C	swim in a pool.	☐

14	If you are under 18, you	A	can only go to Shapers with an adult.	☐
		B	can join a special fitness programme.	☐
		C	need permission from your parents.	✔

15	With the special one-day pass, you can	A	visit any branch of Shapers.	✔
		B	only visit your local branch of Shapers.	☐
		C	have lunch in the Shapers snack bar.	☐

Tip

Sometimes one of the speakers will ask something which clearly introduces an answer. For example, in this part Hillary asks 'What kinds of fitness programmes are available at Shapers?'

If you've underlined the key words in both the question stem and the options, you'll quickly recognise that the man's response will contain the answer to question 13.

Part 4

Questions 16 – 20

You will hear a woman ordering a pizza.

Listen and complete questions **16 – 20**.
You will hear the conversation twice.

Pizza Veneto

Number of pizzas:		*Two*
Type of pizza:	**16**	Special
Free:	**17**	salad
Delivery address:	**18**	...30 / thirty.... *York Avenue*
Floor:	**19**	4th / fourth
Name:	**20**	*Doris* ......Hough.......

Tip

It Helps to Think Ahead (Parts 4 and 5)

Before you listen ...

As you look at the headings in the left-hand column of Parts 4 and 5, make a quick mental note of the kind of information you need to listen for.

Ask yourself: Which questions require numbers? Which require street numbers and/or street names? Which might require a surname the speaker will spell out?

This will prepare you for the details you need to listen for.

TRY IT! - Look at questions 16-20 and 21-25, and answer the questions.

Which question requires ....

1 a closing or opening time? ......21......
2 a long series of numbers? ......23......
3 the number in an address? ......18......

4 one or more days of the week? ......22......
5 an ordinal number (e.g.,1st, 2nd)? ......19......
6 a surname the speaker may spell? ......20......

Part 5

Questions 21 – 25

You will hear some information about a doctor's surgery.

Listen and complete questions **21 – 25**.
You will hear the information twice.

DOCTOR'S SURGERY

Name of doctor:		*Dr Alan Kindy*
Surgery hours:	**21**	*8.30 am* - ....*6.30 pm*....
Surgery days:	**22**	Monday - Friday / Monday to Friday
Number to call at weekends:	**23**	08198 655321
Emergency treatment:	**24**	.....*Eastside*.... *General Hospital*
Special clinics:	**25**	.....*stop smoking*.... *clinic, healthy heart clinic*

You now have 8 minutes to write your answers on the answer sheet.

Listening Spotlight 3

Audioscript on pages 157-158.

Parts 1, 4 and 5 often include questions that test numbers. To answer correctly, you must identify the key words in the question, and then listen for the information that relates to them.

For items 1 – 6, read the questions and underline the key words. Then listen to the speakers and fill in the correct numbers.

1	Which gate number does the flight leave from?	........*17*........
2	How much do tickets for adults cost?	£ ....*3.50*......
3	What time does the centre open on Saturdays?	........*9*........ am
4	What time does their flight leave?	........*12.40*........
5	What time did they go to the cinema?	........*7.30*........
6	How long does it usually take him to get home?	........*1*........ hour

Part 1 (5 – 6 minutes)

Questions for Both Candidates

What's your name?
What's your surname?
How do you spell that?
Where do you come from?

Do you work or are you a student?
What do you do/study?
Do you like it?
Why?/Why not?

Questions for Candidate A

Do you like reading books? Why/why not?
Who is your favourite singer?
Where did you go on holiday last year?
Tell me something about the things you like to do on holiday.

Questions for Candidate B

Do you live in a house or a flat?
How often do you go out with your friends?
What are you going to do tomorrow?
Tell me something about your favourite actor/singer/ musician.

Part 2 (3 – 4 minutes)

1   Candidate A, here is some information about a chocolate museum.

Candidate B, you don't know anything about the museum, so ask A some questions about it. Now B, ask A your questions about the museum, and A, you answer them.

[Candidate A looks at Prompt Card 1A on next page]
[Candidate B looks at Prompt Card 1B on next page]

2   Candidate B, here is some information about a farm park.

Candidate A, you don't know anything about the park, so ask B some questions about it. Now A, ask B your questions about the park and B, you answer them.

[Candidate B looks at Prompt Card 2A on next page]
[Candidate A looks at Prompt Card 2B on next page]

Frequently Asked Questions: Speaking (Part 2)

- **What should I do if I don't understand my partner's question?**
  Ask him/her to repeat the question. Be polite. Say something like, 'Could you repeat that, please?'
  If you are still not sure, ask your partner a question that will show him what you don't understand. For example, if your card is about a magazine, say something like, 'Do you want me to tell you the name of the magazine?'

- **What should I do if my partner finds it difficult to form questions?**
  Try to help out. It may make your partner less nervous, and you will make a good impression on the examiners. For example, you could ask a question like, 'Do you want me to tell you about times?'
  Remember: *If your partner finds it difficult to ask questions, this will not affect your mark.*

NOTE: *Questions and answers in red are examples only. Other responses are possible.*

Prompt Card 1A (Candidate A)

Do you like chocolate?

Visit our new Chocolate Museum and learn all about the history of chocolate.

Join our workshop and make your own chocolate.

Visit the 'Chocolate Bar' and choose from dozens of chocolate bars and 20 different chocolate drinks!

The Chocolate Museum
1819 Hendon Road
Open 7 days a week, 10.30 am – 5 pm

Prompt Card 1B (Candidate B)

- ◆ Where?
  B: Where is the Chocolate Museum?
  A: (It's at) 1819 Hendon Road.
- ◆ What / learn?
  B: What can you learn about there?
  A: (You can learn all about) the history of chocolate.
- ◆ What / make?
  B: What can you make there?
  A: (You can make) your own chocolate.
- ◆ Place / eat and drink?
  B: Is there/Has it got a place to eat and drink?
  A: Yes, you can go to the Chocolate Bar. (It has dozens of chocolate bars and twenty different chocolate drinks).
- ◆ Open weekends?
  B: Is it open at weekends?
  A: Yes, it's open seven days a week.

Prompt Card 2A (Candidate B)

Experience life on an English farm at Snowdean Farm Park!

Feed piglets and lambs.

Visit the Farm Shop with its wonderful selection of freshly picked vegetables.

Open daily from 10 am – 5 pm (4 pm in winter)
Admission FREE!

Prompt Card 2B (Candidate A)

- ◆ What / do there?
  A: What can you do there?
  B: You can feed piglets and lambs.
- ◆ What / buy?
  A: What can you buy there?
  B: You can buy (freshly picked) vegetables.
- ◆ When / open?
  A: When is it open?
  B: It's open from 10 am to 5 pm.
- ◆ Closing time / winter?
  A: What time does it close in winter?
  B: It closes at 4 pm in winter.
- ◆ Cost?
  A: How much does it cost?
  B: It's free. / Admission is free.

A SIMILAR BUT DIFFERENT – Use the words in the box to fill in the gaps in each group.

1   **too   very   enough**

a The tea is ....too.......... hot for me to drink.

b Frank is ....very.......... tall. He's almost 6 foot 5!

c Harriet isn't old ......enough....... to drive a car. She's only 15.

2   **discount   offer   sale**

a There's a 10% ......discount..... for members.

b There's a lovely old house for ....sale......... in the next block.

c Don't miss today's special ....offer......... . Buy any shampoo and get a second one free.

d I bought these jeans in the ....sale.......s . They were reduced from £60 pounds to £30.

3   **cost   value   worth**

a Daisy's new coat ....cost.......... over £100!

b My children don't understand the ....value........ of money. They think it grows on trees!

c Those shoes are very nice, but I don't think they're ....worth.......... £150.

4   **next   later**

a The ....next.......... meeting will be on Sunday, 5th May.

b Call me ....later.......... if you want to go to the beach.

5   **every   each**

a Dad gave Frank and me £20 ....each.......... on our birthday.

b The teacher was pleased when ....every.......... pupil in the class did well in the test.

B SPELLING – Circle the spelling error in each sentence and write the word correctly on the right.

1 I am (writting) a letter to Tom at the moment.   writing
2 Jenny used to (leave) in Leeds, but she moved last year.   live
3 Saturday is the (busyest) day of the week for my dad.   busiest
4 Our new (neibourhood) is really nice.   neighbourhood
5 The band's new single was a great (sucess)   success
6 My son Bill hates (vegatables)   vegetables
7 I wonder what the (whether) will be like tomorrow.   weather
8 The doctor's (surgury) was very busy yesterday morning.   surgery

C QUESTIONS – Put the words in order to form questions.

1 museum / there / park / at / a / the / is / car / ?   Is there a car park at the museum?
2 me / can / for / sandwich / you / a / get / ?   Can you get a sandwich for me?
3 in / music / any / there / area / the / shops / are / ?   Are there any music shops in the area?
4 art / Saturdays / open / the / on / is / gallery / ?   Is the art gallery open on Saturdays?
5 start / the / time / does / what / film / ?   What time does the film start?
6 London / to / Chris / go / school / in / does / ?   Does Chris go to school in London?

D **DIALOGUE BUILDING** – Choose the best response.

1 Does George work in a bank?

A No, I don't think he is.
(B) Yes, I think so.

2 Does the restaurant have a car park?

(A) Yes, it's behind the building.
B I'm afraid there aren't any.

3 Can you get me a glass of water, please?

(A) Of course.
B Yes, you can.

4 Are there any public telephones in the building?

A Yes, they are. It's on the first floor.
(B) Yes, there's one on the first floor.

5 Is the museum open on bank holidays?

A No, it's closed next week.
(B) I'm afraid not.

6 What time does the match start?

A Yes, at 8 o'clock.
(B) I'm not sure. Let's check the newspaper.

Follow-up: Discuss the answers. Talk about: (a) why you chose each answer, and (b) why the other answer can't be correct.

E **WRITING SKILLS: Proofreading for Punctuation and Capitalisation**

1 The letter below is full of punctuation and capitalisation mistakes. Rewrite it correctly on the lines provided.

dear karen

i like going to the cinema very much there are two big cinema's in my town i like Mysteries best but i also enjoy comedies and adventure Films

love

zara

Dear Karen,

I like going to the cinema very much. There are two big cinemas in my town. I like mysteries best, but I also enjoy comedies and adventure films.

Love,

Zara

2 Now compare answers with a partner. Discuss any differences you find, and try to agree on a correct solution.

Part 1

Questions 1 – 5

Which notice (**A – H**) says this (**1 – 5**)?

For questions **1 – 5**, mark the correct letter **A – H** on your answer sheet.

Example:

0   ...F....   You can buy music for less here.   *Answer:* | 0 | A B C D E F G H |

---

1   ...D....   You must eat before you take this medicine.

2   ...C....   You can ask someone about a job here.

3   ...H....   You can take this to get to the 5th floor.

4   ...G....   You can clean your car here at no cost.

5   ...A....   You can buy something to eat here.

A SNACK BAR ON 5th FLOOR

B CAR WASH
Wait here when red light is on.

C SALES ASSISTANT REQUIRED.
See manager for details.

D Take two tablets after every meal.

E Make money working from home!
See our website for more information.

F ALL CDS HALF PRICE

G 24-HOUR PETROL STATION
Free car wash

H PASSENGER LIFT
5th Floor Only

Tip

Part 1 often has pairs of signs that have similar phrases but different meanings.

Don't let this confuse you. Always start with the sentence on the left. Underline the key words. Then look through all the signs. If you find two with similar key words, compare them carefully so you can rule one of them out.

TRY IT! - Look at Part 1 again. Answer the questions.

1 Which sentence mentions getting to the 5th floor? ...3...
   Which 2 signs have the phrase '5th floor'? ...A, H...
   Which sign best relates to the sentence? ...H...

2 Which sentence refers to asking about a job? ...2...
   Which 2 signs are about jobs? ...C, E...
   Which sign best relates to the sentence? ...C...

3 Which sentence is about cleaning a car? ...4...
   Which 2 signs mention washing cars? ...B, G...
   Which sign best relates to the sentence? ...G...
   What key words helped you decide?
      In sentence: ....at no cost.........
      In sign: ....free of charge.........

Part 2

Questions 6 – 10

Read the sentences about television and radio.
Choose the best word (**A**, **B** or **C**) for each space.

For questions **6 – 10**, mark **A**, **B** or **C** on your answer sheet.

Example:

0 Janet likes to .... TV before she goes to bed.

(A) watch   **B** look   **C** see

Answer:

---

6 Mike got home late and .... his favourite show.

   A lost   (B) missed   **C** passed

7 I .... comedy shows to documentaries.

   (A) prefer   **B** rather   **C** choose

8 The weather .... said it was going to rain tomorrow.

   (A) forecast   **B** prediction   **C** announcement

9 My neighbour's alarm clock is so .... that it wakes me up every morning.

   A high   (B) loud   **C** strong

10 The news .... on at 10 o'clock every evening.

   A starts   (B) is   **C** turns

Tip

Sometimes the missing word is part of a set phrase called a collocation. When answering questions in Part 2, it's important that you think about how each word is used in combination with other words.

TRY IT! - Underline the words that complete the sentences.

1 I .... the bus yesterday.   <u>missed</u>   lost

   I .... my keys yesterday.   missed   <u>lost</u>

   I .... you yesterday.   <u>missed</u>   lost

2 I .... TV last night.   looked   saw   <u>watched</u>

   I .... a brilliant film yesterday.   looked   <u>saw</u>   watched

   .... at me when I talk to you!   <u>Look</u>   See   Watch

Part 3

Questions 11 – 15

Complete the five conversations.

For questions **11 – 15**, mark **A, B** or **C** on your answer sheet.

Example:

0

What do you do in your free time?

A   I listen to music.

B   The cinema.

C   At weekends.

Answer: | 0 | A ▬ | B ☐ | C ☐ |

11	Can you tell me how to get to the station, please?	A	I don't like trains.
		(B)	Of course.
		C	No, thank you.

12	Do you have this T-shirt in blue?	A	Mine's blue.
		B	I prefer red.
		(C)	Yes, here you are.

13	Would you like to pay by cash or credit card?	A	No, I don't like it.
		B	Yes, I would.
		(C)	Cash, please.

14	Are you busy this weekend?	A	I only work on weekdays.
		(B)	No. Let's go somewhere.
		C	I like to relax.

15	How much is a ticket to Harrogate?	A	Very much.
		B	It's not very far.
		(C)	£15

Tip

Modal verbs like *can, could* and *would* may cause problems in Part 2 because they have a wide range of uses. Another problem is that questions with modals can be answered with a wide range of short answers. Question 13 is a good example. The word *or* signals that the speaker is asking about which of two options the other person prefers. 'Yes, I would' is wrong because it does not express a preference. The answer - 'Cash, please' - does. It's short for: 'I'd like to (I'd prefer to) pay by cash, please.'

Remember: Thinking about the use (or function) of a question will often help you to find the correct response.

TRY IT! - In the items below, TWO options are possible. Put a line through the one that isn't.

1	Would you like to go swimming?	I'd love to.	Sorry, I can't.	~~Yes, I'd like~~
2	Can you answer the phone, please?	Of course.	~~Yes. Can you?~~	I'd be glad to.
3	Could I take tomorrow off?	Yes, you may.	Sorry, you can't.	~~No, you might not.~~
4	Would you like some tea?	~~Yes, I'd like to.~~	I'd love some.	Not just now, thanks.

Questions 16 – 20

Complete the conversation between two friends.
What does Nick say to Anne?

For questions **16 – 20**, mark the correct letter **A – H** on your answer sheet.

Example:

Anne: I hear you're going away next week. Can I record some programmes for you?

Nick: **0**   ....*B*....

Answer:

0	A	B	C	D	E	F	G	H

Anne:	Okay, what's first?	**A**	Good idea! Alan has a really good DVD recorder.
Nick:	**16** ....*F*....		
Anne:	Okay, what's next?	**B**	That would be great! Have you got a pen? I'll give you the times and days.
Nick:	**17** ....*H*....		
Anne:	If you mean the one about China, it's on Wednesday at 9 pm.	**C**	Oh, dear! That's the same time as my favourite series.
Nick:	**18** ....*C*....	**D**	Yes, just after *The News at 10.*
Anne:	Well, I could ask Alan to record the documentary, and I'll record your series.	**E**	There's a quiz show after the film on Monday.
Nick:	**19** ....*G*....	**F**	Let's see ... Yes, I remember. The first one is *Film of the Week*, 7.30 Monday, on Channel 5.
Anne:	It's on at 11 pm, isn't it ?		
Nick:	**20** ....*D*....	**G**	Good idea! And, finally, could you record *International Film of the Week* on Friday night?
Anne:	Of course. Is that everything?		
Nick:	Yes, it is! And thank you. I really appreciate it!	**H**	When is that documentary that we read about in the TV guide?

Think about it!

In the middle of the dialogue (just before item 18), Anne suggests that their friend Alan could record one programme and she could record the other. How does Nick respond? Compare options A and G, both of which begin with 'Good idea!' Both are possible if you consider what's *before* the gap, so how do you decide which is correct?

Remember: The option you choose must also make sense with what's *after* the gap. Option A says the idea is good and then explains why. Option G says the idea is good, then moves the dialogue forward by moving on to the next programme that Nick wants Anne to record. Which fits in better with what Anne says next? ....Option G........

Part 4

Questions 21 – 27

Read the article about Sudoku and then answer the questions.

For questions **21 – 27**, mark **A, B** or **C** on your answer sheet.

SUDOKU
The 200-Year-Old Puzzle

Sudoku, the popular puzzle that uses the numbers 1 – 9, might not be very new. According to some websites, Sudoku is based on the work of Leonard Euler, an 18th-century Swiss mathematician. Euler created 'Latin Squares', a grid in which every number or symbol appears once in each row or column.

9				8	2	6
	6					4	1
		1		2			7
6			1			8	
		8				1	
	7			4			9
4				8		6	
7	1					2	
	3	6	2				4

In the 1970s a series of puzzles called 'Number Place' appeared in a puzzle magazine by an American publisher. The puzzles were similar to Euler's 'Latin Squares': every number could be used only once in each row or column. In 1984 a Japanese publisher saw the puzzles and was impressed: he made them easier, called them 'Sudoku' (meaning 'single number' in Japanese) and published them in a book. The puzzles continued to appear in the American magazine and in Japanese books, but nobody showed much interest in them.

That began to change in 1997 when Wayne Gould, a New Zealander working in Hong Kong, saw a Sudoku book in a bookshop and was fascinated by it. In October 2004 he persuaded *The Times* to publish one of the puzzles.

It was an instant success … and now you can find Sudoku puzzles in most British newspapers, on the Internet, and even on mobile phones. There are also monthly Sudoku magazines and even a Sudoku puzzle on BBC Radio 4's *Today* programme, where the numbers are read aloud.

Example:

0	Leonhard Euler was	(A)	a maths expert.
		B	a web site designer.
		C	a computer programmer.

Answer:

0	A	B	C

21	Number puzzles were first printed in the United States	A (B) C	in the 1700s. in the 1970s. in 1984.
22	The American publisher called the puzzles	A B (C)	'Euler's Squares'. 'Latin Squares'. 'Number Place'.
23	When the puzzles first appeared in Japan, they were	A B (C)	not hard enough. not called Sudoku at first. easier than the American puzzles.
24	Between 1984 and 2004, the puzzles	A B (C)	became very popular in the USA. became very popular in Japan. existed, but were not very popular.
25	In 1997 Wayne Gould was working	(A) B C	in Hong Kong. in a book shop. for a newspaper.
26	Wayne Gould convinced *The Times*	A B (C)	to publish a Sudoku book. to buy a Sudoku book. to include a puzzle in the paper.
27	The BBC	A (B) C	has a TV programme about Sudoku. has a Sudoku puzzle on the radio. gives solutions to newspaper Sudoku puzzles.

Tip

One way to check yourself on Part 4 is to approach each question as if it were three 'True or False' statements: stem + option A; stem + option B; stem + option C. The reason why this is such a good technique is simple. It forces you to check the stem and all three options carefully until you are sure that two options are wrong and one is right.

Here's an example. Look at question 21. If you read the stem too quickly and see only the phrase 'were first printed', you might think 'A' is true. Then you go to the second statement. You read the stem again and suddenly you notice the phrase 'in the United States'. You check the text against the stem and 'B', and you see that this option is true. This forces you to change your mind about 'A'. You then check the stem and 'C', and you see that it's false. You have now identified two false statements and one true statement ... so you know for sure that 'B' is the answer!

Part 5

Questions 28 – 35

Read the article about Gibraltar.
Chose the best word (**A, B,** or **C**) for each space.

For questions **28 – 35**, mark **A, B** or **C** on your answer sheet.

Gibraltar

Over 5 million people visit Gibraltar every year. **(0)** ………
little bit of Britain in Spain is only eight square kilometres
and has a population of 3,000, but it has three large
yacht marinas and miles of beautiful beaches.

Gibraltar is very much like Britain. It has the famous red
telephone boxes; Gibraltar police wear the **(28)** ……….
uniforms as British police; the money **(29)** ………. the
same; and the people speak English. The only real difference is the climate.

People travel **(30)** ………. all over Europe to shop on Gibraltar because it is tax free, so things
are **(31)** ………. cheaper there.

(32) ………. out on Gibraltar is also amazing. You can find everything from British-style pubs to
Spanish *tapas* bars and from fish and chips to paella. There are so many bars and restaurants
(33) ………. you could stay for a whole year and never eat at the same place twice.

As well as shopping, eating and sunbathing, there are plenty of other things to do on Gibraltar.
You **(34)** ………. visit one of the many historical sites or, if you're feeling adventurous, why not try
scuba diving or a dolphin safari?

And you don't need to wait until summer to visit Gibraltar. Even in winter, the **(35)** ………. rarely
drops below 20° centigrade.

Language Note

On Gibraltar

You may have noticed that the preposition *on* is used when talking about Gibraltar. There are two possible
explanations for this.

First, Gibraltar is a rock 426 metres high. People think of it as a mountain and residents often refer to
themselves as living 'on the rock'.

Second, Gibraltar is a British colony at the southernmost tip of the Iberian peninsula. It is surrounded on
three sides by water, and the remaining side forms the border with Spain. This border was closed from
1969 to 1982, which effectively made Gibraltar an 'island'. Hence the use of the preposition *on*.

Example:

0	(A) This	**B** These	**C** A

Answer: | 0 | A B C |

28   **A** similar   **B** alike   (C) same

29   **A** are   (B) is   **C** be

30   **A** to   (B) from   **C** by

31   (A) much   **B** very   **C** more

32   **A** Eat   **B** Eaten   (C) Eating

33   **A** than   (B) that   **C** which

34   **A** would   **B** will   (C) can

35   **A** weather   **B** thermometer   (C) temperature

Think about it!

Part 5: More Common Question Types

- **Words that introduce clauses (question 33)**   than   that   which

All of the choices are words that usually fit into longer sentences which have a main clause and a dependent clause. Items like this require you to look at both parts of the sentence and try to figure out how the two parts are related. Think about when you would usually use the choices, then look for clues in the main clause. For example: Has the main clause got a comparative which would require *than* to introduce the second part? Is there a phrase beginning with *so* or *such* that requires *that* to introduce a clause of result? Does the main clause end in a noun which is followed by a relative clause that gives you more information about the noun?

- **Modal verbs in context (question 34)**   would   will   can

When you're faced with choosing between three modal verbs, you need to go back to the text and think carefully about the meaning of the sentence you're trying to complete. Ask yourself questions like: Is the gapped word part of a conditional sentence? Is the sentence a prediction about the future? Does it talk about present or future ability?

Part 6

Questions 36 – 40

Read the descriptions of things you can find in your bathroom.
What is the word for each one?

The first letter is already there. There is one space for each other letter in the word.

For questions **36 – 40**, write the words on your answer sheet.

Example:

0   You put soap on this when you are having a bath or shower.   s <u>p</u> <u>o</u> <u>n</u> <u>g</u> <u>e</u>

Answer: | **0** | *sponge* |

---

36   This is a liquid that you use when you wash your hair.   s <u>h</u> <u>a</u> <u>m</u> <u>p</u> <u>o</u> <u>o</u>

37   This usually comes in a tube and you use it to clean your teeth.   t <u>o</u> <u>o</u> <u>t</u> <u>h</u> <u>p</u> <u>a</u> <u>s</u> <u>t</u> <u>e</u>

38   You look at yourself in one of these when you comb your hair.   m <u>i</u> <u>r</u> <u>r</u> <u>o</u> <u>r</u>

39   This is something you can put on your hair after you wash it.   c <u>o</u> <u>n</u> <u>d</u> <u>i</u> <u>t</u> <u>i</u> <u>o</u> <u>n</u> <u>e</u> <u>r</u>

40   You stand on these to see how much you weigh.   s <u>c</u> <u>a</u> <u>l</u> <u>e</u> <u>s</u>

Tip

- Sometimes the word you try to fill in may be too short because you have forgotten a 'silent' letter – that is, a letter which is written but not pronounced. Look at example (0). The 'e' at the end of *sponge* is an example of a silent letter.

- You might also misspell a word with a vowel sound that sounds like one letter but is actually two: for example, *kangaro* or *kangaru* instead of *kangaroo*.

TRY IT! - Look at your answers to questions 36 – 40.

1 Find 2 more words with a silent -*e*.   ...toothpaste...   ...scales......

2 Find 3 words with a vowel sound   ...shampoo...   ...toothpaste...   ...conditioner...
       made up of 2 letters.

Part 7

Questions 41 – 50

Complete this letter.
Write ONE word for each space.

For questions **41 – 50**, write the words on your answer sheet.

Example: | **0** | *on* |

Dear Helen,

I was wondering if you could meet me after school **(0)** ....*on*....... Friday. I want **(41)** ....*to*........ get Ginny a present for her birthday. I'm not sure what to buy for **(42)** ....*her*....... , though.

I know she **(43)** .....*listens*.... to music a lot, so I might buy her a CD. I know which singers she likes, but I **(44)** ....*am*....... afraid she might already have all **(45)** ......*their*...... CDs. Perhaps you could **(46)** ......*find*...... out for me. If she **(47)** ......*has*....... got them all, maybe you could think of **(48)** .*something*. else I could buy her.

We could meet **(49)** ....*at*........ 5.30 outside the college. **(50)** ......*Let*...... me know if you can come.

Love,

Barbara

Tip

Verb Alert!
When you finish Part 7, always read through the passage and check that the words you've filled in make sense. Remember to check before and after each gap.

Then read through a second time to make sure that any verbs you've filled in are in the right form.

Remember to:

- Check before the gap to see if there is an auxiliary verb or modal that will affect your choice.
- Check the subject to make sure you've used the form that goes with it: e.g., base form or base form + -s in the Present Simple; *have* or *has* for Present Perfect.
- Check the surrounding sentences to make sure you've used a form that makes sense in context.

Part 8

Questions 51 – 55

Read the information about a talk at a local town hall.
Complete Sue's notes.

For questions **51 – 55**, write the information on your answer sheet.

ALAN SALES

(author of *Neighbourhood Watch*)

**will be giving a talk at the Town Hall
about keeping your home safe.**

Saturday, 9th April, 11am,
in the Committee Room.

Morning coffee will be served.

Dear Sue,

There has been a change of plan. Alan's talk next Saturday will be two hours later, at 1 pm. This is a bit late for morning coffee, so we will be serving lunch instead.

Also, there is going to be a council meeting in the Committee Room so Alan's talk will be in the Concorde Room, instead.

Can you ring Colin at 'The Advertiser' and ask him to print the changes, please?

Thanks,

Kenny

SUE'S NOTES

Subject of talk:		Keeping your home safe.
Name of person to ring:	**51**	Colin
Original meeting place:	**52**	Committee Room
New meeting place:	**53**	Concorde Room
New time:	**54**	1 pm
Refreshments:	**55**	lunch

Part 9

Question 56

Read this note from your English pen-friend Karen.

I saw a brilliant detective film last night at the cinema. Do you like going to the cinema? Are there many cinemas in your town? What kind of films do you like?

Karen

Write a note to Karen. Answer the questions.

Write 25 – 35 words.

Write the note on your answer sheet.

Tip

Before you begin, list the points you must write about:

1 Do I like going to the cinema?

2 How many cinemas are there in my town?

3 What kind of films do I like?

Use this list to check your answer:

Have you ...

• written about all 3 points?

• used a closing phrase such as 'Regards' or 'Best wishes'?

• signed your name?

• proofread for grammar, spelling and punctuation?

• checked your word count?

Dear Karen,

I like going to the cinema very much. There are two big cinemas in my town. I like detective stories like you, but I also enjoy watching comedies and adventure films.

Love,

Hilda

35 words

Part 1

Questions 1 – 5

You will hear five short conversations.
You will hear each conversation twice.
There is one question for each conversation.
For questions **1 – 5**, put a tick (✔) under the right answer.

Example:

0   How many students are there in the language class?

9	10	15
A ✔	B ☐	C ☐

---

1   How does Alan usually get to work?

A ☐	B ✔	C ☐

2   Where will they go on their anniversary?

  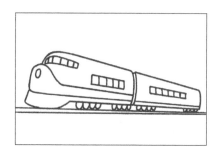

A ✔	B ☐	C ☐

3   What time will Frank arrive?

9 am	1.30 pm	2.30 pm
A ☐	B ☐	C ☑

4   Which woman is Elaine's English teacher?

 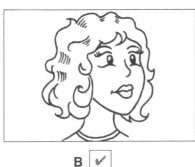 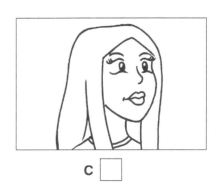

A ☐	B ☑	C ☐

5   How much did Brian pay for his jacket?

£75	£100	£25
A ☑	B ☐	C ☐

Tip

Part 1 often has an item based on the description of a person. If the pictures are "head" shots (as in question 4), the answer will usually depend on your understanding words related to hair. For example:

> length - *short, long, medium-length, shoulder-length*
> colour - *fair, blond(e), grey, dark, light*
> type - *curly, wavy, straight*
> style - (women only) *fringe, pony-tail, pig tails, plaits* (or *braids*)

If the pictures are of men, words like *bald, beard, moustache, goatee,* and *clean-shaven* might also be used.

TRY IT! - Look at the pictures in question 4. Which woman (A, B or C) has ...
>   long, straight hair? ..C..   medium-length, straight hair? ..A..   medium-length wavy hair? ..B...

Part 2

Questions 6 – 10

Listen to a couple talking about their friends' taste in films.
Which kind of film does each of their friends like?

For questions **6 – 10**, write a letter (**A – H**) next to each person.
You will hear the conversation twice.

Example:

0   Adam   B

---

6   John   G

7   Jenny   C

8   Dennis   F

9   Sally and Fred   H

10   Jane   E

A	Thrillers
B	Detective stories
C	Love stories
D	Comedies
E	Documentaries
F	Adventure films
G	Science fiction
H	Historical films

Tip

Before you listen ...
Always cross out the option used in the example, so you're not tempted to use it again.

As you listen ...

Remember: The information on the recording is always in the same order as the questions. You will find it easier to answer the questions if you listen first for the names or other key words in the left-hand column. Then shift your focus to the choices on the right as the speakers continue to talk.

Use the second listening to check your answers and fill in anything you missed the first time.

Part 3

Questions 11 – 15

Listen to Pauline talking to a man in a shop about some furniture she has ordered.

For questions **11 – 15**, tick (✔) **A**, **B** or **C**.
You will hear the conversation twice.

Example:

0	Pauline ordered the furniture from	A	the shop.	✔
		B	a website.	
		C	over the phone.	

11	Pauline placed the order on	A	Monday.	✔
		B	Tuesday.	
		C	Thursday.	

12	The table she received is	A	brown.	
		B	black.	✔
		C	white.	

13	The chairs are	A	missing.	
		B	the wrong colour.	✔
		C	broken.	

14	The man in the shop offers to	A	change the table.	
		B	paint the chairs.	
		C	change the chairs.	✔

15	Pauline wants the shop to	A	replace the furniture.	
		B	refund her money.	✔
		C	complain to the delivery company.	

> **Tip**
>
> **Different Words, Same Meaning**
>
> Expect one or two questions on Part 2 to contain options that rephrase language you hear on the recording. The words you hear will be different than the correct option, but the meaning will be the same.
>
> There is a good example of this in question 15. On the recording, Pauline says: 'What I want is my money back!' The correct option (B) uses different language to say the same thing: the phrase 'refund her money' means 'give her back her money'.

Part 4

Questions 16 – 20

You will hear a man registering with an employment agency.

Listen and complete questions **16 – 20**.
You will hear the conversation twice.

Tempos Employment Agency
Registration Form

Type of job:		*holiday*
Name:	**16**	*John* ......Sheridan......
Address:	**17**	...30 / thirty... *London Road*
Telephone number:	**18**	0116 310 2538 ....
Jobs:	**19**	*office clerk or* (shop) assistant ....
Money:	**20**	£5.50 / five pounds fifty .... *an hour*

Tip

Commonly Confused Number Alert!

Expect one or more items in Part 4 and 5 to be based on your ability to hear the difference between commonly confused numbers ending in **-teen** and **-ty**: for example, 13 vs. 30, 15 vs. 50 and so on.

After you mark Parts 4 and 5, look back at items 17, 20 and 21. Did you get these correct? If so, you probably don't have a problem in this area! If you did make mistakes, keep the following in mind:

-ty numbers - When speaking at a natural pace, native speakers of English will almost always put a heavy stress on the first syllable, and make the second syllable very short: THIR-ty, FOR-ty, FIF-ty and so on.

-teen numbers - The stress varies from speaker to speaker, but as a general rule, in natural speech neither the first syllable nor the second syllable is as heavily stressed as the first syllable of **-ty** numbers.

If you hear a **heavy stress** in the number, go with the **-ty** number. If you can't hear a noticeable stress on either syllable, go with the **-teen** number.

Part 5

Questions 21 – 25

You will hear some information about something that was found on a bus.

Listen and complete questions **21 – 25**.
You will hear the information twice.

Lost Property Report

Found item: *book*

	21	Number ...seventeen / 17....
Bus:

From: 22   ....Ashton...... bus station

Time: 23   twenty past eight / 20 past 8 / 8.20

Type of book: 24   *paperback*

Name of book: 25   ....French.... for Beginners

You now have 8 minutes to write your answers on the answer sheet.

Listening Spotlight 4

Audioscript on page 158.

Part 3 requires you to listen for factual information. To answer correctly, you must identify the key phrase or phrases in each question, and then listen for the information that relates to it.

Read each question and underline the key words. Then listen to each speaker and underline the answer.

1	When will they visit Pisa?	Wednesday	Monday	Friday
2	He will buy his son a	book	pen	CD
3	Which place will the tour visit last?	gardens	castle	museum
4	He booked a room at the	Midland	Imperial	Palace
5	When is Alan's birthday?	Saturday	Thursday	Friday
6	She would like to visit	Greece	France	Austria

Part 1 (5 – 6 minutes)

Questions for Both Candidates

What's your name?
What's your surname?
How do you spell that?
Where do you come from?

Do you work or are you a student?
What do you do/study?
Do you like it?
Why?/Why not?

Questions for Candidate A

Do you like reading books? Why/why not?
Who is your favourite singer?
Where did you go on holiday last year?
Tell me something about the things you like to do on holiday.

Questions for Candidate B

Do you live in a house or a flat?
How often do you go out with your friends?
What are you going to do tomorrow?
Tell me something about your favourite actor/singer/ musician.

Part 2 (3 – 4 minutes)

1   Candidate A, here is some information about an Internet café.

Candidate B, you don't know anything about the Internet café, so ask A some questions about it. Now B, ask A your questions about the Internet Café and A, you answer them.

[Candidate A looks at Prompt Card 1A on next page]
[Candidate B looks at Prompt Card 1B on next page]

2   Candidate B, here is some information about a castle.

Candidate A, you don't know anything about the castle, so ask B some questions about it. Now A, ask B your questions about the castle and B, you answer them.

[Candidate B looks at Prompt Card 2A on next page]
[Candidate A looks at Prompt Card 2B on next page]

Do's and Dont's

Watch your body language!

- DO look at the examiner and show that you are listening to what he or she is saying by nodding your head or saying 'Yes'.

- DON'T put your head down or cover your mouth with your hand. This makes it hard for the examiner and the other candidate to hear what you are saying.

NOTE: *Questions and answers in red are examples only. Other responses are possible.*

Prompt Card 1A (Candidate A)

NET INTERNET CAFÉ

12 London Road

SPECIAL OFFER:

Surf the net for free every Saturday

between 9 am and 12 noon!

Large selection of drinks and snacks

Opening times: 9 am – 9 pm
7 days a week.

Prompt Card 1B (Candidate B)

◆ Name?
B: What is the name of the Internet café?
A: (The name is/it's called) Net Internet Café.

◆ Where?
B: Where is it?
A: (It's at)12 London Road.

◆ Open/Sundays?
B: Is it open on Sundays?
A: Yes, it is.

◆ Cost/Saturday morning?
B: How much does it cost on Saturday mornings?
A: It's free.

◆ Eat/drink?
B: Can I get anything to eat and drink? / Is there anything to eat and drink?
A: Yes, you can./Yes, there is. There's a large selection of drinks and snacks.

Prompt Card 2A (Candidate B)

SANDFORD CASTLE

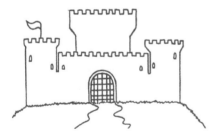

Getting there: The castle is at Junction 19 of the M6 just outside Marford.

Admission: Adults: £10.00
Under 18s/students: half price
Open: 9 am – 12 noon daily

There is so much to see at Sandford.
Don't forget to buy a guidebook at the Ticket Office.
See our website for more information:
www.sandcastle.uk

Prompt Card 2B (Candidate A)

◆ Where?
A: Where is the castle?
B: At Junction 19 of the M6 just outside Marford.

◆ Cost/adults?
A: How much does it cost for adults?
B: £10.00

◆ Open/afternoon?
A: Is/Does it open in the afternoon?
B: No it isn't./doesn't.

◆ Where/guidebook?
A: Where can I get/buy a guidebook?
B: (You can get/buy one) from the Ticket Office.

◆ Information?
A: Where can I get more information?
B: From the website (www.sandcastle.uk)

A **SIMILAR BUT DIFFERENT** – Use the words in the box to fill in the gaps in each group.

1 look   see   watch

a How many hours a day do you ....watch........ television?

b ....Look........ ! The kitten has climbed to the top of the tree again!

c Granddad's eyesight is getting worse. He can hardly ....see.......... anything now.

2 lost   missed   passed

a Eric got home late and ....missed........ his favourite TV programme.

b Rose ......passed....... all the other runners and won the race.

c I've ....lost.......... my ring. Can you help me to find it, please?

3 high   loud   strong

a I wish my neighbours wouldn't turn the volume on their TV up so ....high.......... .

b That woman's voice was really ....loud..........! I could hear her in the next room!

c That was a really ....strong........ wind last night. It blew two of our trees down.

4 like   similar

a Jane and Doreen often wear ....similar........ clothes.

b Jane often wears clothes ....like.......... Doreen's.

B **PREPOSITION PRACTICE** – Use the words in the box to fill in the gaps in the sentences.

about   for   to   with

1 Helen works ....for.......... an advertising agency.

2 Please remember to ask your teacher ....about........ the trip.

3 I read ....about........ the accident in the newspaper.

4 We'll start today's lesson ....with.......... a film about pollution.

5 Have they found a solution ....to.......... the problem yet?

6 Can you record tonight's film ....for.......... me, please?

7 What are you two talking ....about........ ?

8 Some people enjoy listening ....to.......... classical music.

C **QUESTIONS** – Put the words in order to form questions about a party.

1 your / son's / is / when / birthday / ?   When is your son's birthday?

2 a / party / having / he / is / ?   Is he having a party?

3 people / many / how / invited / he / has / ?   How many people has he invited?

4 it / is / be / to / going / where / ?   Where is it going to be?

5 a / yet / bought / him / you / present / have / ?   Have you bought him a present yet?

6 with / who / are / going / you / ?   Who are you going with?

D **DIALOGUE BUILDING** – Complete the conversation between Ellen and Lynn. For each gap, write the question (**A – H**) that best fits in each gap. The first has been done as an example.

Ellen: **0** ......*F*.......

Lynn: Yes. In fact, it's next Saturday.

Ellen: **1** ......*C*.......

Lynn: Of course, we are. We always do something nice for the occasion.

Ellen: **2** ......*H*.......

Lynn: We're having a party.

Ellen: **3** ......*D*.......

Lynn: All of our friends. There'll be about twenty of us.

Ellen: **4** ......*E*.......

Lynn: We thought about having it at our house, but it's a bit small. In the end, we decided to book the party room at the new Chinese restaurant.

Ellen: **5** ......*B*.......

Lynn: They're too young to stay out late, so we've arranged for a baby-sitter. Say, if you're not doing anything on Saturday, why don't you come?

A	Are your friends Eve and Ed coming?
B	Are you bringing your children?
C	Are you going to celebrate?
D	How many people have you invited?
E	Where is it going to be?
F	Isn't it your anniversary soon?
G	Do you have a big house?
H	What are you going to do?

E **WRITING SKILLS – Proofreading for Correct Grammar**

1 Janie has problems with verbs. Circle her errors and correct them on the right. If a line has no error, put a tick (✔).

Dear Sandy,

You know I am enjoying shopping. My lessons will finished at 4 on Friday, so I could to meet you at 4.30. Let's meet outside the bus station, won't we? See you Friday.

Janie

enjoy
....
will finish
....
meet
....
✔
....
shall
....

2 Mike has problems with prepositions. Circle his errors and correct them on the right. If a line has no error, put a tick (✔).

Dear Sandy,

I'd love to go shopping with you at Friday. I finish my last class to 3 o'clock so I could meet you on front of the train station at 3.30, across of the bank.

Mike

✔
....
on
....
at
....
in
....
from
....

Part 1

Questions 1 – 5

Which notice (**A – H**) says this (**1 – 5**)?

For questions **1 – 5**, mark the correct letter **A – H** on your answer sheet.

Example:

0 ...*F*.... Children under 5 must be with an adult.

Answer:

0	A	B	C	D	E	F	G	H
	—	—	—	—	—	▬	—	—

1 ...G... You cannot get your money back.

2 ...A... Dinner is cheaper before 5 o'clock.

3 ...B... Things will be cheaper until this Friday.

4 ...E... You can get a snack or beverage here on Wednesday morning.

5 ...H... You can get a passport here.

A
> **EARLY-BIRD SPECIAL 4-5 pm**
> 1/3 off on all meals

B
> **Sale ends on Friday**

C
> **PASSPORT CONTROL**
> Please have your passport ready.

D
> **SPECIAL OFFER:**
> Buy two, get one free every Friday.

E
> **COFFEE BAR**
> Closed for repairs Wednesday afternoon

F
> No under 5s admitted
> without an adult.

G
> **No refunds under
> any circumstances.**

H
> **PASSPORT OFFICE**
> Applications 9 am – 5 pm daily

Tip

Questions in Part 1 are often based on your ability to recognise different ways of talking about times, days of the week, and numbers like prices or ages.

Always start with the sentences. Read carefully, and underline key words such as days, numbers, prices and ages. Also underline words or phrases that go with these, e.g., *before/after, from ... to, until/by, morning/afternoon, over/under, more than, less than*. Then look for the sign (or signs) with similar key words, compare carefully with the sentence, and choose the best answer.

TRY IT! - Look at Part 1 again. Answer the questions.

1 Which sentence mentions Friday? ...3...
Every Friday or a specific Friday? ..a specific Friday..
Which 2 signs have the word 'Friday'? ...B, D...
Which sign best relates to the sentence? ...B...

2 Which sentence has the number 5? ...2...
Is it a time, a price or an age? ...a time...
What other key word goes with the number? ..before..
Which signs have the number 5? A, F, H
Which signs refer to 5 pm? ..A, H..
Which sign best relates to the sentence? ...A...

Part 2

Questions 6 – 10

Read the sentences about going to a restaurant.
Choose the best word (**A, B** or **C**) for each space.

For questions **6 – 10**, mark **A, B** or **C** on your answer sheet.

Example:

0 My favourite .... of food is Spanish.

    (A) kind   **B** variety   **C** choice

Answer: 

---

6 I usually take my friends out for a .... on my birthday.

    A dinner   **B** food   (C) meal

7 Frances .... all her friends to the restaurant.

    (A) invited   **B** called   **C** requested

8 After we had looked at the menu, the waiter came back and .... our orders.

    A served   **B** gave   (C) took

9 This is the best restaurant I've .... been to.

    A always   (B) ever   **C** already

10 We ordered roast chicken and potatoes for the .... course.

    (A) main   **B** major   **C** chief

Tip

Sometimes the answer depends on the situation (or context). In question 8, for example, you must think about what happens in a restaurant right after you look at the menu. Two of the options (A and C) fit the structure of the sentence, but only one suits the situation.

TRY IT! - Read each sentence carefully. Think about the context, then underline the answer.

1 When we sat down, the waiter brought us the	fork	bill	<u>menu</u>	
2 After we'd decided what to eat, he .... our order.	served	<u>took</u>	brought	
3 A few minutes later, he .... our starters.	<u>served</u>	ordered	cooked	
4 At the end of the meal, we ordered	bill	<u>dessert</u>	vegetables	
5 The service was excellent, so we left the waiter a nice	receipt	bill	<u>tip</u>	

Part 3

Questions 11 – 15

Complete the five conversations.

For questions **11 – 15**, mark **A, B** or **C** on your answer sheet.

Example:

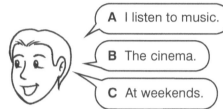

0

What do you do in your free time?

A I listen to music.

B The cinema.

C At weekends.

Answer:

0	A	B	C
	▬	☐	☐

11 What time shall I pick you up?

    A Yes, please!
    (B) At 7 o'clock.
    C Here!

12 It's cold in here.

    A Shall I close it?
    B Not yet!
    (C) Yes, it is.

13 Can I borrow your umbrella?

    (A) Yes, of course.
    B I'll put it down.
    C It was a real bargain!

14 The last bus is at 11 pm.

    A Is it near the station?
    B That's not enough.
    (C) That's a bit early!

15 Where do you live?

    A All my life.
    B A room at the hotel.
    (C) In Grange Street.

Tip

When in doubt, work backwards!

If you're not sure of an answer, it sometimes helps to work backwards from the choices.

- First, look at the question or comment on the left, and think about the situation.
- Then look at each option and ask yourself: What question would I expect to find if this were the answer?

Think about the situations. Then write a question for each choice. (2 of the answers are the questions in 11 and 15.)

1 **A friend is arranging to pick you up.**
   Yes, please. - ......Shall I pick you up?.........
   At 7 o'clock. - ....What time shall I pick you up?...
   Here! - ......Where shall I pick you up?...

2 **You meet someone. He asks about your home.**
   In Grange Street. - ....Where do you live?.........
   All my life. - ...How long have you lived there?...
   In a room at the hotel. - ......Where are you staying?.....

Questions 16 – 20

Complete the conversation.
What does Audrey say to Bill?

For questions **16 – 20**, mark the correct letter **A – H** on your answer sheet.

Example:

Audrey: Hello, Bill. What are you doing here?

Bill: **0** ....B.....

Answer:

Audrey: I'm looking for a present for my mum, too. Any ideas?

Bill: **16** ....D.....

Audrey: Great idea. She loves jewellery.

Bill: **17** ....F.....

Audrey: I think I know it. Is it next to the cinema?

Bill: **18** ....H.....

Audrey: Let's go and see what they have.

Bill: **19** ....E.....

Audrey: Do you think your mum will help me to choose something?

Bill: **20** ....G.....

Audrey: Brilliant. See you at the jeweller's!

A	I'm not very good at choosing presents.
B	Hi, Audrey. Actually, I'm looking for a present for my mum.
C	My mum buys a lot of jewellery there.
D	How about a watch?
E	I'm waiting for my mum now, but we can meet you there in about 20 minutes.
F	My mum does, too. Her favourite jeweller's is the one in Mount Street.
G	I'm sure she'll be delighted to help.
H	Yes, that's the one. They have some really nice watches.

Tip

Check yourself!
When you've filled in all the gaps, always read through the dialogue to make sure each answer makes sense. Remember to check before and after the gap.
Some things to check for:
- Requests for suggestions (*Any ideas?*) are followed by a suggestion (e.g., *Why don't you ... ? / How about ... ?*).
- Suggestions/invitations (*Let's ... / Shall we ...? / Would you like to ...?*) are followed by a positive reaction (*Great idea!*) or a new suggestion (*I'm doing something now, but ...*).
- Request for opinions (*Do you think she ...?*) are followed by an opinion (*I'm sure she ....*).

Part 4

Questions 21 – 27

Read the article about Hutt River Province in Australia.
Are sentences **21 – 27** 'Right' **(A)** or 'Wrong' **(B)**?
If there is not enough information to answer 'Right' **(A)** or 'Wrong' **(B)**, choose 'Doesn't say' (C)

For questions **21 – 27**, mark **A, B** or **C** on your answer sheet.

The Second Biggest Country in Australia

The biggest country on the continent of Australia is, of course, Australia (population, 20.5 million). According to Leonard Casely, Hutt River Province (population, 60) is the second biggest. Casely, an Australian farmer, decided to start his own 'country' after a disagreement with the Australian government in 1970. Hutt River Province (HRP) is 595 miles north of Perth in Australia. It is ruled by 'Prince' Leonard and his wife, 'Princess' Shirley.

HRP has a small church, an art gallery, a post office, a motel, a shopping centre and a campsite. It also has its own coins, notes and postage stamps, all of which have pictures of Prince Leonard on them. The province gets most of its money from selling sheep, wool and wild flowers. It also receives money from tourism. About 30,000 people visit HRP every year, mostly to buy stamps and to have their picture taken with Prince Leonard and Princess Shirley or other members of the HRP royal family.

Despite the fact that HRP is not officially recognised as a country, it has ambassadors in France, Norway, Estonia, Madagascar, the Vatican, New Caledonia, Singapore, Spain, Russia, Scotland, Jersey and, of course, Australia. If you want to become a citizen of HRP, just apply to Prince Leonard. You won't be alone: over 13,000 people, living all over the world, have HRP passports!

Example:

0   More than 20 million people live in Australia.

(A) Right   **B** Wrong   **C** Doesn't say   *Answer:*

---

21   The Australian government wanted to buy Casely's farm in 1970.
A Right   **B** Wrong   (C) Doesn't say

22   HRP is in Perth, Australia.
A Right   (B) Wrong   **C** Doesn't say

23   Hutt River Province has its own money.
(A) Right   **B** Wrong   **C** Doesn't say

24   Hutt River Province gets most of its income from tourism.
A Right   (B) Wrong   **C** Doesn't say

25   HRP sells 30,000 stamps every year.
A Right   **B** Wrong   (C) Doesn't say

26   Twelve countries officially recognise HRP as a country.
A Right   (B) Wrong   **C** Doesn't say

27   Anyone can become a citizen of HRP.
(A) Right   **B** Wrong   **C** Doesn't say

Tip

Watch out for statements in the questions that refer back to sentences in the text with *Despite ...* , *Despite the fact that ...* , *Although ...* , *Even though*. Remember that these linking words and phrases always occur in sentences that express a contrast or conflict between two facts in the sentence:

one thing is or is not true   *but*   a second thing is also true

Question 26 is a good example of how tricky things can get. The question relates back to the first sentence of the final paragraph. You go back and count the countries at the end of the first sentence ... and you find that there are exactly 12 countries mentioned. 'Great!' you think. 'The answer is "right".' But look again! The second part of the sentence clearly states that those 12 countries have ambassadors, but the first part states just as clearly that HRP is *not* officially recognised as a country. Therefore, the statement is 'wrong'.

Part 5

Questions 28 – 35

Read the article about making phone calls.
Choose the best word (**A, B,** or **C**) for each space.

For questions **28 – 35**, mark **A, B** or **C** on your answer sheet.

Phoning Home

Until fairly recently, people in **(0)** ………. parts of the world had to spend days travelling to the capital city or the **(28)** ………. large city just to make a phone call.

John Daily, **(29)** ………. works for the charity 'Village Support', first went to Cameroon, West Africa, **(30)** ………. 2002. At that time there were just over 100,000 telephones in Cameroon, a country with more than 17 million people.

'When I first got here, I had to take two days off work to go into Yaounde, the capital, to phone **(31)** ………. family in the UK,' says Daily. 'When I finally got there, I had to wait in a long queue to book a call. Then I waited again, often for several hours, before the call **(32)** ………. connected. Most of the time the line was so bad that I could hardly **(33)** ………. the person at the other end, or I would be cut off after only a few minutes.'

Now mobile phones have arrived in Cameroon and things have changed. '**(34)** ………. aren't any antennas in the village where I'm **(35)** ………., so I still have to go into town when I want to use my mobile phone. But at least I don't have to wait in a long queue anymore, and I can always hear the person at the other end!'

Example:

0	(A) some	**B** all	**C** every		*Answer:*	0	A B C

28   (A) nearest   **B** nearer   **C** near

29   **A** where   **B** which   (C) who

30   (A) in   **B** to   **C** at

31   **A** his   **B** their   (C) my

32   (A) was   **B** is   **C** be

33   **A** listen   (B) hear   **C** speak

34   **A** Their   (B) There   **C** They

35   **A** works   **B** work   (C) working

Think about it!

Verbs patterns (question 33)   **listen**   **hear**   **speak**

All three verbs might appear in a paragraph that talks about having problems with phone calls, but in this case only one of the verbs fits the structure of the sentence. Which is it?

Remember: Some verbs in English can be followed by a preposition + object; others are followed by a direct object without a preposition. In this case, there is an object after the gap but no preposition, so you must find the verb that can be used in this pattern.

TRY IT! - Fill in the gaps with the correct form of *listen, hear* or *speak*. Remember to 'mind the gap'!

1   Of course I'm ....listening....... to you, but the line is bad and I can't ....hear.......... you. I always ....listen......... when someone ....speaks....... to me! It's the polite thing to do!

2   Last week John was ....speaking...... at a business conference. Suddenly, his microphone went dead and no one could ....hear.......... him. It was just as well. They hadn't been ....listening...... anyway! They had ....heard.......... so many speeches over the past week that some people felt that they never wanted to ....listen.......... to another speech ever again!

Part 6

Questions 36 – 40

Read the descriptions of words about food.
What is the word for each one?

The first letter is already there. There is one space for each other letter in the word.

For questions **36 – 40**, write the words on your answer sheet.

Example:

0   This tells you how to make something to eat.   r e c i p e

Answer: | 0 | recipe |

---

36   This is something sweet you eat after a meal.   d e s s e r t

37   This is the meal you eat in the morning.   b r e a k f a s t

38   These are the things you need to make a meal.   i n g r e d i e n t s

39   This is what you eat before the main course in a restaurant.   s t a r t e r

40   This is what we call two slices of bread with meat,   s a n d w i c h
cheese, etc., between them.

Do You Remember?

Look at the definitions in questions 36 – 40.

1   Which require a singular? ....36, 37, 39, 40.......

2   Which require a plural? ....38...............

If you don't remember how to determine this, look back at the Tip on page 18.

Part 7

Questions 41 – 50

Complete these notes.
Write ONE word for each space.

For questions **41 – 50**, write the words on your answer sheet.

Example: | 0 | *the* |

Mike,

I'm going to (0) ..*the*..... University Open Day with Janet next weekend, but I'm not really sure how to get (41) ..there.. . I know I catch the number 27 bus from the station, (42) ...but... I'm not sure where to get (43) ...off.... or how to get to the university (44) ..from.. the bus stop. Please send me the directions.

Charlotte

Charlotte,

Ask the driver to tell you (45) ..when. you get to Sedgley Park. If you follow the path through the park, you (46) ...will... see the university in (47) ..front.. of you. The Open Day Welcome Meeting is usually (48) ....in.... the lecture theatre, (49) ..which. is on the second (50) ..floor.. .

Mike

Tip

Remember:

- When you complete all the gaps, read your work over carefully to see if the grammar is correct and your answers fit the meaning of the text(s).

- Check the verbs you've filled in. Are they in the right form?

- Finally, check your spelling. Think carefully about any words you may have filled in that are commonly confused (e.g., *there/their/they're; its/it's, which/witch*)

Part 8

Questions 51 – 55

Read these two notes about having something repaired.
Complete Elaine's notes.

For questions **51 – 55**, write the information on your answer sheet.

Dear Sarah,

I'll call round on Friday afternoon on my way from the gym to look at your washing machine. I should be there at around 2 pm.

If it's just the door, I'm sure I'll be able to óx it. We had a similar problem with our tumble dryer a couple of months ago.

See you on Friday.

John

Elaine,

John wants to come to my flat tomorrow at 2 pm to repair the washing machine.

I know you're meeting him at the tennis club tonight, so can you ask him to come on Saturday instead? I have to take Kevin to football practice, but I will be back by 2.30.

Also tell him I can get the door to close now, but it still won't switch on.

Thanks,

Sarah

ELAINE'S NOTES

Talk to:		John
Where:	**51**	tennis club
Repair:	**52**	Sarah's washing machine
Problem:	**53**	won't switch on
Day:	**54**	Saturday
Time:	**55**	2.30 pm

Part 9

Question 56

Read this note from your English pen-friend Janet.

> I'm happy that your brother Tim is coming to visit us. Please tell me where and when to meet him and what he looks like.
>
> Janet

Write a note to Janet. Answer the questions.

Write **25 – 35** words.

Write the letter on your answer sheet.

Tip

Before you begin, list the points you must write about:

1   where to meet Tim ....

2   when to meet Tim ....

3   what Tim looks like ....

Use this list to check your answer:

Have you ...

• written about all 3 points?

• used a closing phrase such as 'Regards' or 'Best wishes'?

• signed your name?

• proofread for grammar, spelling and punctuation?

• checked your word count?

QUESTION 56: MODEL ANSWER

Janet,

It would be great if you'd meet my brother at the coach station at 10 on Sunday morning. He is tall and slim, and he has short brown hair and blue eyes.

Regards,
Leanne

35 words

Part 1

Questions 1 – 5

You will hear five short conversations.
You will hear each conversation twice.
There is one question for each conversation.
For questions **1 – 5**, put a tick (✔) under the right answer.

Example:

0   How many students are there in the language class?

9	10	15
A ✔	B ☐	C ☐

1   Which table does the man like?

A ☐   B ☐   C ✔

2   What time does Mary's party start?

A ✔   B ☐   C ☐

3 Where will Tina go on holiday?

A ☐   B ☐   C ✔

4 What has the man lost?

A ☐   B ☐   C ✔

5 How much does one ticket cost?

£50	£15	£7.50

A ☐   B ✔   C ☐

Tip

The Shape of Things

Sometimes a question will depend on your knowledge of nouns and adjectives related to shapes.

Question 1 is a good example. The speakers mention the phrases 'square dining table with chairs around it' and 'small rectangular coffee table'. Your task is to listen and choose the picture that matches the description which answers the narrator's question.

Match the words and shapes.

1 square - square
2 circle - round
3 triangle - triangular
4 oval - oval
5 rectangle - rectangular

Part 2

Questions 6 – 10

Listen to Anita talking to John about shopping.
What is John going to buy from each shop?

For questions **6 – 10**, write a letter (**A – H**) next to each shop.
You will hear the conversation twice.

Example:

0	chemist's	E

6	supermarket	G
7	baker's	D
8	newsagent's	H
9	greengrocer's	F
10	butcher's	B

A	a birthday card
B	a chicken
C	some lamb
D	a birthday cake
E	a bandage
F	fruit and vegetables
G	toothpaste
H	wrapping paper

Tip

Listen before you leap!

Don't assume that an answer is correct just because it seems logical.

In this exercise, for example, options B and C can both be bought at a butcher's, and options A and H can both be bought at a newsagent's. The speakers discuss all of these options, but Anita asks John to buy only one item at each place.

Remember: Listen carefully to decide which is the correct answer. Use the first listening to answer as many questions as possible, and the second listening to check your answers and fill in anything you missed.

Part 3

Questions 11 – 15

Listen to George asking about computer courses.

For questions **11 – 15**, tick (✔) **A, B** or **C**.
You will hear the conversation twice.

Example:

0	George is interested in a course for	**A**	beginners	✔
		B	advanced learners.	
		C	professionals.	

11	The maximum number of students in the beginners class is	**A**	six.	
		B	four.	✔
		C	ten.	
12	There are evening classes on	**A**	weekends.	
		B	weekdays.	
		C	Wednesdays.	✔
13	The course lasts for sixty	**A**	days.	
		B	hours.	✔
		C	weeks.	
14	If you pay in full when you enrol, the course costs	**A**	less.	✔
		B	more.	
		C	the same.	
15	The best time to enrol is	**A**	mornings.	
		B	lunchtime.	
		C	afternoons.	✔

Tip

Expect at least one item in your test booklet to present you with language that you do not hear in the dialogue. When this happens, you need to think carefully about what the speakers are saying ... and then look for the option that expresses this idea in different words.

Question 14 is a good example of this. The woman does say 'If you pay for the whole course when you enrol, it's only £42, instead of £60'. The question stem and one of the options express this idea using slightly different words.

Remember: If you fail to answer such a question on the first listening, don't panic. Look carefully at the stem and underline the key words or phrases. On the second listening, listen carefully for words or phrases on the recording that mean the same as the key words you've underlined. Then read all three options and choose the one that best summarises the meaning of what you've heard.

Part 4

Questions 16 – 20

You will hear a man booking a taxi.

Listen and complete questions **16 – 20**.
You will hear the conversation twice.

BRADFORD CABS
Customer Pick-Up Form

Name of customer:		Bill Lanford
Day:	**16**	....Thursday...., 26th June
Time:	**17**	5 am /five am
Address:	**18**	16 ....Manshaw.... Road
Going to:	**19**	....Terminal 2...., Manchester Airport
Phone number:	**20**	310 1408

| **Tip** |

Spelling on Parts 4 and 5: When Does It Count?

On Parts 4 and 5, you're expected to spell common words like months and days of the week correctly. Correct spelling is also required on any words that the speakers spell out. In this test, for example, you'd be expected to use correct spelling for items 16, 18 and 24.

Recognisable (though incorrect) spelling would be acceptable in items like 19 and 22, where the words are not as common.

Part 5

Questions 21 – 25

You will hear some information about an excursion.

Listen and complete questions **21 – 25**.
You will hear the information twice.

Excursion Notes

Visit to:	Roman Villa and Gardens

Opening times:

21	...10 am – 5 pm... *daily*

Meeting point for tour:

22	*outside the* Villa (villa) entrance

Last tour:

23	4/four pm

Price of admission:

24	free / free of charge

Price of tour:

25	£4.50/four pounds fifty

You now have 8 minutes to write your answers on the answer sheet.

Listening Spotlight 5

Audioscript on page 158

In Parts 4 and 5 you are asked to listen to a dialogue or monologue and then write down information that is missing from a set of notes. In some questions, the answers are common words that you are expected to spell correctly. This exercise gives you examples of some of these words.

Listen and fill in the missing information.

1 Snack bar: ....sandwiches....   5 Closed on: ....Saturdays....
2 Courses start: ....February....13th   6 Next course: ....October...... 2006
3 Meet at: ....theatre......   7 Moved: last ....winter....
4 Item bought: ....DVD player....   8 Starter: ....chicken soup....

Part 1 (5 – 6 minutes)

Questions for Both Candidates

What's your name?
What's your surname?
How do you spell that?
Where do you come from?

Do you work or are you a student?
What do you do/study?
Do you like it?
Why?/Why not?

Questions for Candidate A

Do you spend a lot of time with your friends? Why/Why not?
What's your favourite restaurant?
What are you going to do next weekend?
Tell me something about your hobbies.

Questions for Candidate B

Do you prefer to spend your birthday with friends or family? Why/Why not?
What presents did you get on your last birthday?
Do you live in a house or a flat?
Tell me something about your country.

Part 2 (3 – 4 minutes)

1   Candidate A, here is some information about a skateboarding competition.

   Candidate B, you don't know anything about the skateboarding competition, so ask A some questions about it. Now B, ask A your questions about the skateboarding competition and A, you answer them.

   [Candidate A looks at Prompt Card 1A on next page]
   [Candidate B looks at Prompt Card 1B on next page]

2   Candidate B, here is some information about a fireworks display.

   Candidate A, you don't know anything about the fireworks display, so ask B some questions about it. Now A, ask B your questions about the fireworks display and B, you answer them.

   [Candidate B looks at Prompt Card 2A on next page]
   [Candidate A looks at Prompt Card 2B on next page]

Tip

- DO try to support your answers with examples. For instance, if the examiner asks you about your favourite restaurant, don't just tell him or her the name, but say something about it. Say something like 'My favourite restaurant is *[name of restaurant]* because it has really delicious food.'

- DON'T stop speaking for so long that the examiner thinks you have finished answering the question when you haven't. If you can't remember a word or you lose your train of thought, say something like 'Just a moment, please.'

NOTE: *Questions and answers in red are examples only. Other responses are possible.*

Prompt Card 1A (Candidate A)

Hilton Park
Skateboarding Competition

Are you free this Saturday?
Do you enjoy skateboarding?

Why not enter our skateboarding competition?
You could win £500.

No special equipment necessary except
your skateboard and a helmet!

The competition starts at 12 noon.

Entry fee: £3.50

Prompt Card 1B (Candidate B)

◆ Where/competition?
   B: Where is the skateboarding competition?
   A: It's in Hilton Park.

◆ When?
   B: When is the skateboarding competition?
   A: It's on Saturday.

◆ Prize?
   B: What is the prize?
   A: (The prize is) £500. / You can win £500.

◆ Equipment?
   B: Is any equipment necessary? / Do I/you
      need any equipment?
   A: Yes, a skateboard and a helmet.

◆ Cost?
   B: How much does it cost?
   A: (The entry fee is) £3.50 (three pounds fifty).

Prompt Card 2A (Candidate B)

BONFIRE NIGHT
FIREWORKS DISPLAY
November 5th

See our amazing fireworks display,
and try traditional Bonfire Night snacks.

Selection of special Bonfire Night
toffees on sale.
Fireworks display starts 8 pm.

Adults: £2.00   Children: £1.00
Family ticket: £4.50

Prompt Card 2B (Candidate A)

◆ When / fireworks display?
   A: When is the fireworks display?
   B: It's on November 5th.

◆ Eat?
   A: Will there be anything to eat? / Can I get
      anything to eat? / What can I eat?
   B: (There will be / You can eat) traditional
      Bonfire Night snacks.

◆ Start?
   A: What time does it start?
   B: (It starts at) 8 pm.

◆ Buy?
   A: What can I buy?
   B: Special Bonfire Night toffees.

◆ Family ticket/cost?
   A: How much is a family ticket?
   B: £4.50 (four pounds fifty).

A SIMILAR BUT DIFFERENT – Use the words in the box to fill in the gaps in each group.

1   her   hers   she's

a I really like Sue. ....She's....... a good friend and a great photographer, too. That photo on the wall is ....hers.......... . It won an award in a photo competition last year.

b Anna's an excellent student. ....Her.......... parents are very proud of her.

2   gone   been

a Ian has ....been........ to Spain twice this year, but he's in London at the moment.

b Ned has ....gone........ to the supermarket. He'll be home soon.

3   anything   something   nothing

a Is there ......anything..... to eat? I'm starving. I've had ....nothing...... to eat since 7 am!

b You must be hungry. I'll make you .....something.... .

4   read   study

a Your vocabulary will improve if you ....read........ books, newspapers and magazines.

b John can't come to the cinema. He has to ....study........ for his French test.

5   prize   present

a Donna won first ....prize......... in the dancing competition.

b I'm looking for a ....present...... for my brother's birthday.

B SPELLING – Circle the spelling mistake in each sentence. Then rewrite the word correctly on the right.

1 Roy had a (dissagreement) with his boss this morning.   ....disagreement...........

2 Jamie's changed so much that I hardly (regognised) him.   ....recognised...........

3 I've never seen such a wide (variaty) of foreign magazines.   ....variety...........

4 The supermarket was so busy I had to wait in the (qeue) for 30 minutes.   ....queue...........

5 Most shops won't give you a refund if you don't have a (reciet). ....receipt...........

6 Norman's absolutely (delited) about winning the prize.   ....delighted...........

7 Flour is one of the main (ingridiants) in most cakes.   ....ingredients...........

8 I'm not good at (chosing) clothes. I never know what to wear.   ....choosing...........

C QUESTIONS WITH *LIKE* – Fill in each gap with a word or phrase from the box.

Do   Does   How do you   What's   What does   What would you   Would you

1 I know Mike likes French food, but ....does............ he like Italian food, too?

2 ....What's........... that new Chinese restaurant like? Is it any good?

3 We're going to the Italian restaurant. ....Would you........ like to come?

4 ....What would you.... like to do tonight?

5 ....Do.............. you like your steak? Mine is delicious!

6 I prefer meat when it's well-done. ....How do you........ like yours?

7 ....What does........ Harvey like more: pizza or burgers?

D **DIALOGUE BUILDING** – Match each question to the appropriate answer. The first has been done as an example.

0	What's the new employee like?	A	Would you? It's very warm in here.
1	How do you like your new job?	B	Would you? They're terribly heavy.
2	What would you like for dinner?	C	She seems quite nice.
3	Would you like me to open the window?	D	A steak and a salad would be lovely.
4	Do you like comedies?	E	I'd love to.
5	Would you like to join us for dinner on Saturday?	F	I love it!
6	Would you like me to help you with those packages?	G	I love them! They're my favourites!

E **WRITING SKILLS** – Identifying and Responding to the Questions in the Writing Prompt

1   The letters below are responses to the same exam question. Two of the candidates have done the task well. The other candidate wrote a letter about a similar topic, but <u>did not include the information the question was asking for.</u> Compare the letters, and answer these questions:

a   Which two are similar?   ......A and C......
b   Which is different?   ....B..........
c   Is the different one well written?   ....Yes..........
d   Would it have got full marks?   ....No..........   (see underlined words above)

A

Dear Penny,

It is expensive to eat out in my city, but there are many good restaurants here. My favourite is called Chiquita. It has Mexican food and it's not too expensive.

Regards,

Geoff

B

Dear Penny,

I don't shop for food, but I think it isn't expensive. I like Greek food. My favourite is chicken and potatoes. My mother cooks it in the oven with lemon. It's really tasty.

Best wishes,

Tim

C

Dear Penny,

Yes, it is quite expensive to eat in restaurants here. I don't often go to restaurants, but my favourite restaurant is Truffles. It serves tasty French food.

Love,

Sue

2   Look at the two letters that are similar. Write the three questions that were in the exam question they answered.

Is it expensive to eat out / eat in restaurants in your town?
Do you have a favourite restaurant? / What's your favourite restaurant?
What kind of food does it have?

3   Your teacher has asked you and your classmates to prepare a poster with advice for next year's KET candidates. Here is the list of tips they came up with. Tick (✔) the ones you would include.

✔ ....   Read the exam question more than once.
✔ ....   Underline the key words in the letter in the exam booklet.
   ....   You will get full marks if you write about all three points in the exam question.
✔ ....   Put a tick in the exam booklet next to each point you must write about.
   ....   Correct grammar and spelling are more important than writing about the three points.
✔ ....   Start your final check by making sure you have written about all three points.

Part 1

Questions 1 – 5

Which notice (**A – H**) says this (**1 – 5**)?

For questions **1 – 5**, mark the correct letter **A – H** on your answer sheet.

Example:

0 ...*H*... This is less expensive because it is not new.   *Answer:*

0	A	B	C	D	E	F	G	H
	▭	▭	▭	▭	▭	▭	▭	▬

1 ...*B*... You can pay here if you're only buying a few things.

2 ...*A*... You can't watch a play here in July or August.

3 ...*F*... You cannot make phone calls here.

4 ...*G*... Do not drive after taking this medicine.

5 ...*E*... In the summer this closes later.

A
> **PALACE THEATRE**
> Closed for the summer
> **Grand reopening September 1st**

B
> **EXPRESS CHECK-OUT**
> Maximum 4 items

C
> Take two tablets before
> you go to sleep.

D
> **MOBILE PHONE SALE**
> Up to 50% off on last year's models

E
> **DEBMORE PARK**
> 9 am – 5 pm (Sep – May)
> 9 am – 9 pm (June – Aug)

F
> **SILENT CARRIAGE**
> Please switch off mobile phones.

G
> **WARNING:**
> This medicine will make
> you feel sleepy.

H
> **COMPUTER MONITOR FOR SALE**
> Slightly used, half price

Tip

Some questions require you to think more deeply about the meaning of a word or phrase. For example, a sentence might mention a season of the year, and one or more signs might refer to a month or months, or a month and/or a season. Reading carefully and underlining all the key words will help you keep things straight.

TRY IT! - Look at Part 1 again. Answer the questions.

1 Which sentence mentions one or more months? .....2.....
   Which sentence mentions a season? .....5.....

2 Which sign mentions a season and a month? .....A.....
   Which sign mentions 2 different ranges of months? .....E.....

3 Which sign matches the sentence with the month? .....A.....
   What key words helped you decide?
      In sentence: can't watch – play – July and August
      In sign: theatre – closed – summer

4 Which sign matches the sentence with a season? .....E.....
   What key words helped you decide?
      In sentence: summer – closes later
      In sign: 9 pm – (June – Aug)

Part 2

Questions 6 – 10

Read the sentences about going to the countryside.
Choose the best word (**A**, **B** or **C**) for each space.

For questions **6 – 10**, mark **A**, **B** or **C** on your answer sheet.

Example:

0   We arranged to .... John at the old farm.

(A) meet   **B** find   **C** take

Answer:

---

6   You must drive carefully when you're on .... country lanes.

(A) narrow   **B** thin   **C** slim

7   We always .... our holidays in the countryside when I was a child.

A passed   (B) spent   **C** made

8   My mum always drives .... in the countryside, as she loves to look at the scenery.

A gently   (B) slowly   **C** softly

9   You don't want to frighten the animals, so you must keep your dog under ....

A command   **B** lead   (C) control

10   My sister is always bored in the countryside. She says there's not .... to do.

(A) enough   **B** plenty   **C** many

Tip

Sometimes the choices are very close in meaning, as in items 6 and 8. If you are not sure of the answer, try to remember contexts where you have met each word. You may be able to get to the answer by ruling out one or more of the choices.

TRY IT! - These items are based on the choices in question 6. Underline the correct answers.

		narrow	slim	thin
1 You can see he's been ill. Look at how .... he is.		narrow	slim	<u>thin</u>
2 This skirt is too .... It will never fit over her big hips!		<u>narrow</u>	slim	thin
3 Mary looks great! She's lost weight and is very .... now.		narrow	<u>slim</u>	thin
4 The opening looked .... , but the cat easily went through it.		<u>narrow</u>	slim	thin
5 There was a .... layer of ice on the lake.		narrow	slim	<u>thin</u>
6 I like my pasta with a .... tomato sauce.		narrow	slim	<u>thin</u>

THINK ABOUT IT! - Complete the questions with *narrow, slim* or *thin*.

What is the opposite of 'wide'? ..narrow..   Which means 'attractively built'? ....slim....
What is the opposite of 'thick' or 'heavy'? ....thin....   Which is a synonym of 'skinny'? ....thin....

Part 3

Questions 11 – 15

Complete the five conversations.

For questions **11 – 15**, mark **A, B** or **C** on your answer sheet.

Example:

0

> What do you do in your free time?

> A   I listen to music.

> B   The cinema.

> C   At weekends.

Answer: 0   A B C

---

11   It gets cool in the mountains, so bring a jacket.
  A   How high is it?
  (B) Good idea.
  C   No, thanks. I'm quite warm.

12   Is it OK if I invite Pauline to the party?
  A   I think she's OK now.
  (B) Sure! She's great fun!
  C   I don't think she's coming.

13   Have you seen Annie's new haircut?
  A   Yes, I saw.
  B   Did she?
  (C) Yes, I have.

14   Has the postman been here yet?
  A   Every day except Sunday.
  (B) I don't think so.
  C   He delivers our letters.

15   I can't find my car keys.
  (A) I'll help you to look for them.
  B   Where are they?
  C   I've found it.

Tip

Sometimes you can get to the answer by comparing the subject and verb tense in the question and choices. For example, the question in item 13 (*Have you seen ...?*) is a *Yes/No* question in the Present Perfect. Of the two options that begin with *Yes*, one is clearly a better choice than the other.

Sometimes a simple pronoun check can lead you to the answer. If all three options include a pronoun (e.g., *them, they, it*), then check back for the noun the pronouns refer to. In question 15, for example, *keys* requires a plural pronoun, so 'C' is clearly wrong. Then consider the meaning of 'A' and 'B': if someone says 'I can't find my keys', it's unlikely that the other person would say 'Where are they?', so 'A' must be the answer.

Questions 16 – 20

Complete the conversation.
What does the receptionist say to Helen?

For questions **16 – 20**, mark the correct letter **A – H** on your answer sheet.

Example:

Helen: Hello, I need a haircut. Do I need to make an appointment?

Receptionist: **0** ...*B*......   *Answer:*

| 0 | A | B | C | D | E | F | G | H |

Helen: Can I come on Thursday morning?

Receptionist: **16** ...E......

Helen: What about Friday afternoon?

Receptionist: **17** ...A......

Helen: Anthony does.

Receptionist: **18** ...F......

Helen: That's a bit late. Are you sure there's nothing earlier?

Receptionist: **19** ...G......

Helen: Perfect!

Receptionist: **20** ...D......

Helen: Yes, thank you.

A   Let's see. Who usually cuts your hair?

B   Yes, I'm afraid so.

C   No, of course not.

D   So, we'll see you on Friday.

E   No, sorry. We're fully booked.

F   Yes, Anthony can fit you in at 4 pm on Friday.

G   I'll have another look. Ah, yes. How about 2 pm?

H   Do you just want a haircut?

Tip

Did you remember to:

- read the dialogue first to get a feel for what it is about?
- underline the key words in the dialogue on the left and the options on the right?
- make sure each answer fits with what is *before* and *after* the gap?
- read the completed dialogue through to make sure all your answers make sense?

Part 4

Questions 21 – 27

Read the article about François-Eugène Vidocq and then answer the questions.

For questions **21 – 27**, mark **A**, **B** or **C** on your answer sheet.

THE FIRST DETECTIVE

Who was the first modern detective: Sherlock Holmes? Hercule Poirot? Actually it was someone very few people have heard of: a Frenchman called François-Eugène Vidocq.

Vidocq was born on 24 July 1775. He was always getting into trouble, so his family made him join the army when he was 17. Unfortunately, things didn't get any better: at the age of 20, Vidocq went to prison for the first time.

Soon Vidocq became a skilful criminal. He escaped from prison so many times that he became very well-known. Finally, he decided to change. He went to the chief of police and offered to become a police spy. The chief agreed. Vidocq helped the police to catch so many thieves and murderers that the chief asked him to form a team of 'detectives'.

Vidocq was the first person to employ female detectives. His team had an equal number of men and women. He was also the first investigator to use methods which the police still use today: he and his team worked 'undercover', pretending to be members of criminal gangs. They also used blood samples and fingerprints. Soon they were catching thousands of criminals a year.

In the 19th century Vidocq predicted that in the future 'the scientist will be an even greater enemy to the criminal than the police'. In the 21st century his prediction has finally come true.

Tip

Did you remember to:

*   read the passage first to get a feel for what it's about?
*   read the choices and underline the key words?
*   refer back to the passage to check for the information in each choice?
*   check yourself by seeing whether each choice is True or False?

Example:

0	Who was the first modern detective?	**(A)**	François-Eugène Vidocq	

B   Sherlock Holmes

C   Hercule Poirot   *Answer:*

---

21   When Vidocq was 20, he

     A   got into trouble with his parents.
     (B)   was put in jail for the first time
     C   was forced to become a soldier.

22   Vidocq became famous for

     (A)   escaping from prison.
     B   changing his name.
     C   stealing from people.

23   Who did Vidocq go to when he decided to change?

     (A)   the chief of police.
     B   a spy.
     C   a famous policeman.

24   Who suggested that Vidocq help the police?

     A   the chief of police
     (B)   Vidocq.
     C   a clever police officer.

25   The first team of detectives had

     A   more men than women.
     B   more women than men.
     (C)   as many women as men.

26   Vidocq's methods

     A   are used by teams of criminals.
     (B)   are used by modern police forces.
     C   are used to take blood samples.

27   According to the writer, Vidocq's prediction about scientists

     A   came true in the 1800s.
     B   may soon come true.
     (C)   has already come true.

Part 5

Questions 28 – 35

Read the article about celebrating birthdays.
Choose the best word (**A, B,** or **C**) for each space.

For questions **28 – 35**, mark **A, B** or **C** on your answer sheet.

Another Year Older

What do **(0)** ………. do on your birthday? Have a party and **(28)** ………. your friends? Blow
out some candles? Open presents? Well, if you lived in another country, things might be a little
different. For example, in China **(29)** ………. celebrates their birthday on New Year's Day, even
if it is not their official date of birth. They **(30)** ………. another year older on New Year's Day.
(31) ………. you lived in Russia, your teacher would give you a present at school. Teachers give
pupils gifts such **(32)** ………. flowers, pencils or books to celebrate their **(33)** ………. birthdays.
Your classmates might make a small gift for you, **(34)** ………. .

If you are worried about people forgetting your birthday, you should follow the Dutch tradition.
Most Dutch homes have a calendar in the bathroom to **(35)** ………. friends and relatives of
family birthdays.

Example:

0 Ⓐ you	**B** they	**C** we

Answer: | 0 | A ▬ | B ▭ | C ▭ |

---

28   **A** invited   **B** inviting   Ⓒ invite

29   Ⓐ everyone   **B** nobody   **C** anyone

30   **A** have   Ⓑ turn   **C** go

31   **A** When   **B** Because   Ⓒ If

32   **A** like   Ⓑ as   **C** that

33   Ⓐ students'   **B** student's   **C** students

34   Ⓐ too   **B** to   **C** two

35   **A** reminds   **B** reminding   Ⓒ remind

Tip

Did you remember to:

• read the passage through to get a feel for the overall meaning?

• think about what is being tested in each question (e.g., verb form, quantity words, linking words, possessives, words that sound alike but have different spellings)?

• check that each answer fits both the structure of the sentence and the meaning of the surrounding sentences?

• read the completed passage to see if your answers make sense?

Part 6

Questions 36 – 40

Read the descriptions of buildings.
What is the word for each one?

The first letter is already there. There is one space for each other letter in the word.

For questions **36 – 40**, write the words on your answer sheet.

Example:

| 0 | This is where you go if you want to watch a film. | c i n e m a |

Answer: | **0** | *cinema* |

| 36 | This is a very tall building. | s k y s c r a p e r |

| 37 | People are kept here if they break the law. | p r i s o n |

| 38 | You can look at things from the past here. | m u s e u m |

| 39 | You can keep your money here. | b a n k |

| 40 | This was built for a king or queen to live in. | c a s t l e |

Tip

Spell check!
Remember that correct spelling is essential in this part of the exam. You will not receive marks for words that are spelt incorrectly. Here are some things you can do to avoid making careless mistakes.

- When you copy the words you have found onto your answer sheet, take a few seconds to check that you have copied the words correctly.
- Remember that you must write the **full word** on your answer sheet: e.g., *cinema* (not *inema*).
- Take a few seconds to count the letters of each word you wrote in your test booklet. Then make sure that the word you have written on your answer sheet has the same number of letters.

  Of course, this does not guarantee that you've spelt the word correctly, but it will guarantee that you didn't leave anything out or add anything when you transferred the word onto your answer sheet.

Part 7

Questions 41 – 50

Complete this letter.
Write ONE word for each space.

For questions **41 – 50**, write the words on your answer sheet.

Example: | **0** | about |

Dear sirs,

I am writing (0) ....*about*..... some computer software (41) ......that..... I ordered from your website a week (42) ......ago...... . Unfortunately, I have had a problem (43) .....with....... the disk you sent me.

(44) When/After. the disk arrived, I put it (45) ....in........ my computer and (46) ...nothing... happened. I checked the label and realised (47) ......that...... it was an older version that cannot be used with my computer.

I need the software for my studies, (48) ......so........ I would be grateful if you could write to me (49) ....as........ soon as possible and tell me (50) .....how...... to get the right disk.

Yours faithfully,

Mary Spooner

Tip

Did you remember to:

- read the passage through to get a feel for the overall meaning?

- think about the kind of word missing in each gap (e.g., verb, preposition, linking word, time word, pronoun, part of a common phrase or expression)?

- check the words before and after the gap to make sure your answer fits the structure of the sentence?

- check the surrounding sentences to make sure your answer fits the meaning of the paragraph?

- read the completed passage again to check that all your answers make sense?

Part 8

Questions 51 – 55

Read the information about a photo competition.
Complete David's notes.

For questions **51 – 55**, write the information on your answer sheet.

THE DAILY NEWS
PHOTO COMPETITION

Win a digital camera!

Take your photos into any newsagent's, or bring them to our offices in Crown Road.

Closing date: 21st March

Entry fee: £1.00 per photo

All entrants will receive a free 1-megabyte memory card.

Dear June,

Did you see the ad for the photo competition in 'The Daily News'? You could send the photos you took last July. The ones of the turtles are great, but I think the two dolphin photos are even better.

All you have to do next is to take them to any newsagent's. (You could take them to the newspaper, but it's a bit far). There's one on Bridge Street, just round the corner from the Post Office.

If you enter both photos, you'll need to give the newsagent θ2.00.

Good luck!

David

JUNE'S NOTES

Sponsor:		The Daily News
Closing date:	**51**	21st March
Cost per photo:	**52**	£1 / one pound
Prize:	**53**	(a) digital camera
Photos to enter:	**54**	dolphins
Where to enter:	**55**	newsagent's in Bridge Street

Part 9

Question 56

Read this letter from your English pen-friend Sarah.

> Hi!
>
> I'm really excited because we are going on a school trip to a theme park next week. Where do you go on school trips in your country? How often do you go? What was your favourite school trip?
>
> Sarah

Write Sarah a letter. Answer the questions.

Write **25 – 35** words.

Write the letter on your answer sheet.

Tip

Before you begin, list the points you must write about:

1   Where do we go on school trips?
2   How often do we go on school trips?
3   What was my favourite school trip?

Use this list to check your answer:

Have you ...

• written about all 3 points?
• used a closing phrase such as 'Regards' or 'Best wishes'?
• signed your name?
• proofread for grammar, spelling and punctuation?
• checked your word count?

QUESTION 56: MODEL ANSWER

Dear Sarah,

We usually go to museums on school trips. We take one trip every year. One year we went on a trip to a museum with dinosaurs. It was my favourite trip.

Love,

Fiona

33 words

Part 1

Questions 1 – 5

You will hear five short conversations.
You will hear each conversation twice.
There is one question for each conversation.
For questions **1 – 5**, put a tick (✔) under the right answer.

Example:

0   How many students are there in the language class?

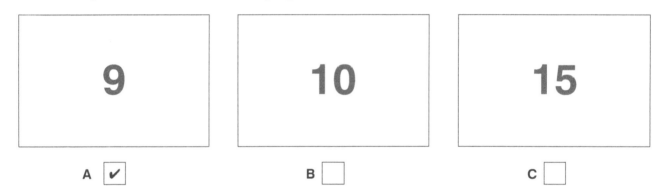

A ✔   B ☐   C ☐

1   What is the man going to do at the weekend?

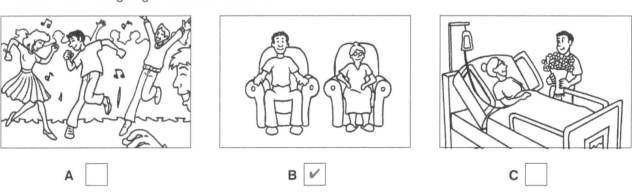

A ☐   B ✔   C ☐

2   How much did the woman's ticket cost?

A ☐   B ☐   C ✔

3   What are they going to have for dinner?

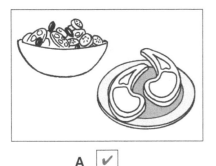  

A ✔   B ☐   C ☐

4   What kind of mirror is the woman looking for?

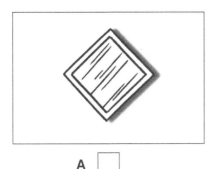 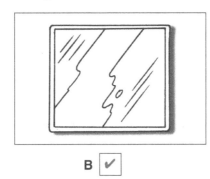 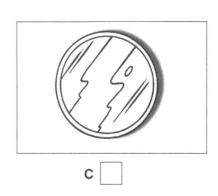

A ☐   B ✔   C ☐

5   What time is the first train to London?

A ☐   B ☐   C ✔

Tip

Even if you think you've heard the answer, don't stop listening!

Sometimes the answer to a question includes more than one piece of information. One detail may come out early in the dialogue, and then another may come out later.

Question 3 is a good example of this. The speakers decide early on that they will have a salad for dinner ... but then the man suggests they have steak as well. After a short discussion of other foods, the woman agrees. If you had stopped listening after they agreed on the salad, you would have ticked the wrong answer.

Remember: Always listen to the whole dialogue before choosing your answer. Use the first listening to fill in as many answers as possible and the second to check your answers and fill in anything you've missed.

Part 2

Questions 6 – 10

Listen to Will talking to Katherine about the gifts she bought in a charity shop.

Who got which gift?

For questions **6 – 10**, write a letter (**A – H**) next to each person.
You will hear the conversation twice.

Example:

0	Irene	H

6	Mick	G	**A**	t-shirt
7	June	C	**B**	sketchpad
8	Anne	F	**C**	cup
			D	pen
9	Sarah	E	**E**	diary
10	Tom	B	**F**	calendar
			G	poster
			H	hat

Tip

Which comes first: the name on the left or the detail on the right?

The names, places or other information that you see in the left-hand column are always in the same order that they are mentioned on the recording. Most of the time you will hear the item in the left-hand column first, followed by the answer in the right-hand column.

Sometimes, however, the item on the right is mentioned *before* you hear the item on the left. For example, in this conversation Katherine tells us what she has bought for **Mick (6)**, and then she says: 'It has the same picture as the **cup (C)** I bought for his girlfriend **June (7)**.'

It's easy to miss this on the first listening, so when you hear the recording a second time, remember to listen carefully to what is said *before* the item you missed.

Part 3

Questions 11 – 15

Listen to a tour guide talking to a woman tourist about a local market.

For questions **11 – 15**, tick (✔) **A**, **B** or **C**.
You will hear the conversation twice.

Example:

0	The first market at Ashbridge began in	A	1289.	✔
		B	1869.	☐
		C	1960.	☐

11	The market didn't open	A	when it was too cold.	☐
		B	when it was too hot.	☐
		C	when it rained.	✔

12	Nowadays the market closes on	A	Sundays.	✔
		B	Fridays.	☐
		C	Tuesdays.	☐

13	You can buy used goods at	A	the European market.	☐
		B	the flea market.	✔
		C	the normal market.	☐

14	The European market	A	is held every four days.	☐
		B	lasts for four days.	☐
		C	is held every Friday.	✔

15	You can get a hot meal	A	at the outdoor market.	☐
		B	in the shopping centre.	✔
		C	In the market hall.	☐

Tip

Before you listen ...

Use the 20-second pause *before* the recording to locate questions you think might be especially tricky. For example, question 14 contains options that look very similar. If you don't read them carefully, you have less of a chance of answering correctly. What should you do?

A good strategy is to circle the words that are similar, and underline the words that are different. Then think about how the meanings differ. This will help you focus your listening on the finer details when the recording is played.

> A (is held) every (four days).
> B lasts for (four days).
> C (is held) every Friday.

Part 4

Questions 16 – 20

You will hear a man registering as a volunteer.

Listen and complete questions **16 – 20**.
You will hear the conversation twice.

Keep Britain Clean
Volunteer Profile

Project:		*Clean Up the Park*
Name:	**16**	John Phillips
Phone number:	**17**	0770 234 5115
Age:	**18**	*turns ....19........ next month*
Available:	**19**	every weekend / weekend(s)
Transport to park:	**20**	free bus

Tip

Parting Advice (Parts 4 and 5)

Before you listen ...

- Remember to use the pause before the recording is played to study the form or notes in your test booklet.
- Underline the key words (name, date, address, and so on) to fix the information you must listen for firmly in your mind.

As you listen ...

- Remember that the information on the form is in the same order as the information on the recording. If you realise you've missed something the first time you listen, don't panic. (If you do, you may miss the next piece of information as well!)
- Use the second listening to check your answers and fill in anything you missed the first time.

Part 5

Questions 21 – 25

You will hear a some information about a recording studio.

Listen and complete questions **21 – 25**.
You will hear the information twice.

Annex Recording Studios
Notes

Location:		*199 Oxford Road*
Available for hire:	**21**	*keyboards, guitars* ......*and drums*......
How to book:	**22**	*complete* ......*online*...... *booking form*
Minimum booking:	**23**	one/1 hour
Cost:	**24**	..£35/thirty-five pounds.. *per hour*
Other features:	**25**	coffee bar

You now have 8 minutes to write your answers on the answer sheet.

Listening Spotlight 6

Audioscript on page 158.

In Parts 4 and 5 of the Listening paper you are asked to listen to the recording and write down information that is missing from a set of notes. This exercise gives you practice in listening for specific information in an extended conversation or monologue. Remember to listen carefully for numbers and for words that are spelt out.

Listen to a man and woman arranging a delivery. Fill in the form.

1 To: ......Jennings...... Motors
   Address: ..11 Station Road..
   Contact: Tom Smith
   Day: ..Tuesday..

2 Time: before ..12 (noon)..
   Sender: ..Wally Weymouth..
   Phone: ..0778 312 5469..
   Cost: £ 5.15...

Part 1 (5 – 6 minutes)

Questions for Both Candidates

What's your name?
What's your surname?
How do you spell that?
Where do you come from?

Do you work or are you a student?
What do you do/study?
Do you like it?
Why?/Why not?

Questions for Candidate A

What is/was your favourite subject at school? Why?
How many people are there in your family?
What's the best place you've ever visited?
Tell me something about your friends.

Questions for Candidate B

What hobbies or activities do you like doing in your free time?
Which countries would you like to visit someday? Why?
Who was the last person you bought a gift for?
Tell me something about your home.

Part 2 (3 – 4 minutes)

1   Candidate A, here is some information about a holiday.

Candidate B, you don't know anything about the holiday, so ask A some questions about it.
Now B, ask A your questions about the holiday and A, you answer them.

[Candidate A looks at Prompt Card 1A on next page]
[Candidate B looks at Prompt Card 1B on next page]

2   Candidate B, here is some information about a film festival.

Candidate A, you don't know anything about the film festival, so ask B some questions about it.
Now A, ask B your questions about the film festival and B, you answer them.

[Candidate B looks at Prompt Card 2A on next page]
[Candidate A looks at Prompt Card 2B on next page]

Tip

- DO be yourself. It's easier to relax if you don't try to impress the examiners with ideas that you think they want to hear.

- DON'T worry if you make a few mistakes. The examiners are more interested in how you communicate your ideas than whether or not you speak with perfect grammar and advanced vocabulary.

NOTE: *Questions and answers in red are examples only. Other responses are possible.*

Prompt Card 1A (Candidate A)

Summer Sun Holidays

Prices from £200 per adult

Children 5-17: £125

Children under 5: free

Flights from all UK airports
Accommodation in 3- and 4-star hotels

See our website for further information:
www.sshols.co.uk

Prompt Card 1B (Candidate B)

♦ Price/adults?
   B: What's the price for adults?
   A: (The price is) £200

♦ Price/children under 5?
   B: What's the price for children under 5?
   A: Children under five are free.

♦ Fly/from?
   B: Where can I fly from?
   A: (You can fly from) all UK airports.

♦ Accommodation?
   B: What is the accommodation (like)?
   A: Accommodation is in 3- and 4-star hotels.

♦ Information?
   B: Where can I get more information?
   A: From the website (from www.sshols.co.uk).

Prompt Card 2A (Candidate B)

24th ANNUAL FILM FESTIVAL

At the Odeon Film Centre
20th June – 27th June

This year's festival features films by
new European directors.

Screenings daily: 10 am – 10 pm

Admission: £3.50

Prompt Card 2B (Candidate A)

♦ Where?
   A: Where is the Film Festival?
   B: (It's at) the Odeon Film Centre.

♦ Dates?
   A: What are the dates?
   B: From 20th to 27th June.

♦ Films?
   A: What (kind of) films are there?
   B: Films by new European directors.

♦ Time?
   A: What time are the films shown?
   B: 10 am – 10 pm.

♦ Price?
   A: What's the price/How much is it?
   B: £3.50 (three pounds fifty)

A SIMILAR BUT DIFFERENT – Use the words in the box to fill in the gaps in each group.

1   **meet**   **find**

    a   Hurry up! We have to ....meet........... Simon in five minutes.

    b   Have you seen my umbrella? I can't ....find............ it anywhere.

    c   The applicant's CV is impressive. If she's got a nice personality, she'll ....meet........... all our requirement

2   **remember**   **remind**

    a   Can you ......remember....... who starred in that comedy we saw?

    b   Can you ....remind......... Oliver to get some bread on the way home.

    c   I never ....remember........... Dad's birthday. Mum always has to ....remind......... me.

3   **thin**   **slim**

    a   When they found the lost dog, it was so ....thin............ you could see its bones.

    b   If you eat the right foods and get plenty of exercise, you will stay ....slim............ and healthy.

4   **gently**   **slowly**

    a   She picked up the old vase very ....gently.......... because she was afraid it would break.

    b   George spoke so ....softly............ that I could hardly hear him.

5   **enough**   **plenty**

    a   I'm afraid I haven't got ....enough.......... money to pay the bill. Can I pay by credit card?

    b   We haven't got any orange juice, but we've got ....plenty.......... of apple juice.

    c   Is there ....enough......... food for everyone? Yes, there's ....plenty........... .

B PREPOSITIONS – Use the words in the box to fill in the gaps in the sentences below. You will have to use one of the words more than once.

    about   **from**   **into**   **on**

1   I'm looking forward to tomorrow. We're going ....on.......... an excursion with the school.

2   Susan's son Mike is always getting ....into....... trouble.

3   I've studied hard, so I'm not worried .....about...... the exams.

4   I was born ....on........ Monday, 20th March 1994.

5   I've written to the travel company to complain ......about...... the holiday they booked for me.

6   The two men who robbed the bank last year have escaped ......from........ prison.

C QUESTIONS – Use the words in the box to complete the gaps. Then match each question to the appropriate answer. The first one has been done as an example.

    are   **did**   **how**   ~~**was**~~   ~~**what**~~   **when**   **where**   **why did**   **why not**   **would**

0   ......What...... was the hotel like? ......Was....... it near the sea?

1   You didn't like the tour guide? ...Why not.... ?

2   ......How....... was your holiday? ....Did........ you have a good time?

3   ......Would..... you recommend I go there someday?

4   ......When...... did you get back? I thought you were staying longer.

5   ......Where...... are you going next year: Germany, maybe, or Norway?

6   ...Why did... you have to leave so quickly? ....Are........ the children all right?

D   DIALOGUE BUILDING – Complete the conversation between Tom and Jim. For each gap, write the question (**A – G**) that best fits in each gap. Two of the choices will not be used.

Tom: Sorry I didn't call you last night. I had to collect my parents from the airport.

Jim: **1** ....D........

Tom: Yes, it was just a quick five-day trip. Dad couldn't take more time off.

Jim: **2** ....G........

Tom: The south of Italy.

Jim: **3** ....A........

Tom: Dad loved it, but Mum said it was 'just okay'.

Jim: **4** ....C........

Tom: Dad would, but Mum wouldn't!

Jim: **5** ....F........

Tom: They haven't decided yet. You know how they are. They can't seem to agree on anything these days!

A   That's right. Now I remember. And did they enjoy themselves?

B   Why didn't she like it?

C   So they wouldn't like to go there again, would they?

D   Oh, back already, are they?

E   How long were they gone?

F   And where are they going next?

G   Remind me. Where did they go this time?

Follow-up: Now compare answers with a partner. Discuss any differences you have, and see if you can agree on a common solution. Be ready to explain your answers.

E   WRITING SKILLS: Final Check

1   The letter below contains a number of errors in spelling, punctuation and grammar. Write the corrected letter in the space provided.

dear Ellen

my new house is fantastic althought it doesnt has a garden. it's not very near at the City centre. I must to go two school on bus because it's quiet far away

Regards

Mario

Dear Ellen,....

My new house is fantastic although it doesn't have a garden. It's not very near the city centre. I must go to school by bus because it's quite far away.

Regards,...

Mario..

2   Now compare answers with a partner. Discuss any differences you find, and try to agree on a correct solution.

PAPER 1: Reading and Writing - Candidate answer sheet 1 (front)

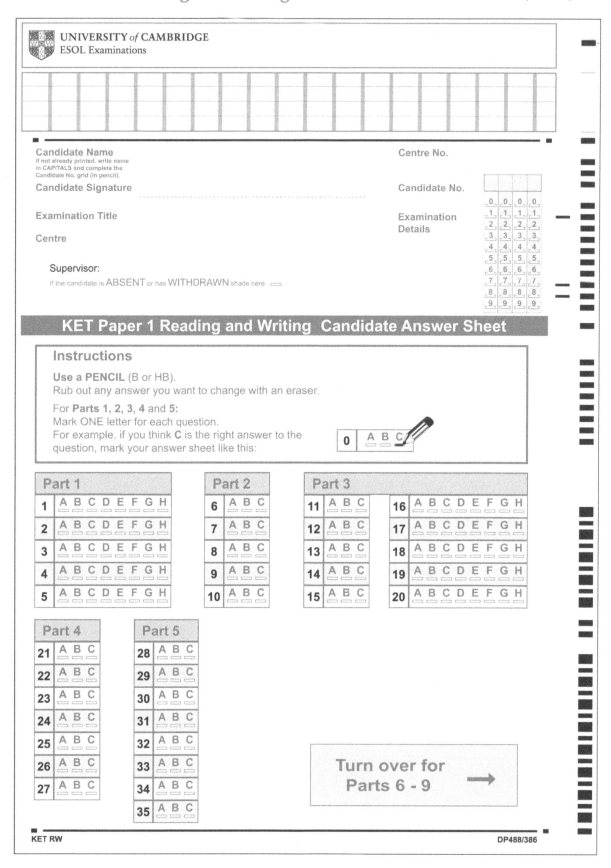

UNIVERSITY of CAMBRIDGE
ESOL Examinations

Candidate Name
If not already printed, write name
in CAPITALS and complete the
Candidate No. grid (in pencil).

Candidate Signature

Examination Title

Centre

Supervisor:
If the candidate is ABSENT or has WITHDRAWN shade here ▭

Centre No.

Candidate No.

Examination Details

KET Paper 1 Reading and Writing Candidate Answer Sheet

Instructions

Use a PENCIL (B or HB).
Rub out any answer you want to change with an eraser.

For **Parts 1, 2, 3, 4** and **5**:
Mark ONE letter for each question.
For example, if you think **C** is the right answer to the
question, mark your answer sheet like this:

0 | A B C

Part 1

1 | A B C D E F G H
2 | A B C D E F G H
3 | A B C D E F G H
4 | A B C D E F G H
5 | A B C D E F G H

Part 2

6 | A B C
7 | A B C
8 | A B C
9 | A B C
10 | A B C

Part 3

11 | A B C
12 | A B C
13 | A B C
14 | A B C
15 | A B C

16 | A B C D E F G H
17 | A B C D E F G H
18 | A B C D E F G H
19 | A B C D E F G H
20 | A B C D E F G H

Part 4

21 | A B C
22 | A B C
23 | A B C
24 | A B C
25 | A B C
26 | A B C
27 | A B C

Part 5

28 | A B C
29 | A B C
30 | A B C
31 | A B C
32 | A B C
33 | A B C
34 | A B C
35 | A B C

Turn over for Parts 6 - 9 →

KET RW

DP488/386

Sample KET answer sheets

PAPER 1: Reading and Writing - Candidate answer sheet 1 (back)

For **Parts 6, 7 and 8:**

Write your answers in the spaces next to the numbers (36 to 55) like this:

0	example

Part 6		Do not write here
36		1 36 0
37		1 37 0
38		1 38 0
39		1 39 0
40		1 40 0

Part 7		Do not write here
41		1 41 0
42		1 42 0
43		1 43 0
44		1 44 0
45		1 45 0
46		1 46 0
47		1 47 0
48		1 48 0
49		1 49 0
50		1 50 0

Part 8		Do not write here
51		1 51 0
52		1 52 0
53		1 53 0
54		1 54 0
55		1 55 0

Part 9 (Question 56): Write your answer below.

Do not write below (Examiner use only)
0   1   2   3   4   5

PAPER 2: Listening - Candidate answer sheet

UNIVERSITY *of* **CAMBRIDGE**
ESOL Examinations

Candidate Name
If not already printed, write name
in CAPITALS and complete the
Candidate No. grid (in pencil).

Candidate Signature

Examination Title

Centre

Supervisor:
If the candidate is ABSENT or has WITHDRAWN shade here

Centre No.

Candidate No.

**Examination
Details**

0	0	0	0
1	1	1	1
2	2	2	2
3	3	3	3
4	4	4	4
5	5	5	5
6	6	6	6
7	7	7	7
8	8	8	8
9	9	9	9

KET Paper 2 Listening Candidate Answer Sheet

Instructions

Use a PENCIL (B or HB).

Rub out any answer you want to change with an eraser.
For **Parts 1, 2** and **3**:
Mark ONE letter for each question.
For example, if you think **C** is the right answer to the
question, mark your answer sheet like this:

0	A B C

Part 1			
1	A B C
2	A B C
3	A B C
4	A B C
5	A B C

Part 2	
6	A B C D E F G H
7	A B C D E F G H
8	A B C D E F G H
9	A B C D E F G H
10	A B C D E F G H

Part 3	
11	A B C
12	A B C
13	A B C
14	A B C
15	A B C

For **Parts 4** and **5**:
Write your answers in the spaces next to the
numbers (16 to 25) like this:

0	example

Part 4		Do not write here
16		1 16 0
17		1 17 0
18		1 18 0
19		1 19 0
20		1 20 0

Part 5		Do not write here
21		1 21 0
22		1 22 0
23		1 23 0
24		1 24 0
25		1 25 0

KET L

DP314/088

Audioscript

TEST 1

Narr: This is the Cambridge Key English Test, Test 1, Paper 2. There are five parts to the test: Parts 1, 2, 3, 4 and 5. We will now stop for a moment before we start the test. Please ask any questions now because you mustn't speak during the test.
Now look at the instructions for Part 1.
You will hear five short conversations.
You will hear each conversation twice.
There is one question for each conversation.
For questions 1 – 5, put a tick under the right answer.
Here is an example:
How many students are there in the language class?
M: Are there many students in your language class?
W: There were ten, but one of them left.
M: That's quite a lot.
W: I know, but last year there were fifteen.
Narr: Now listen again.
The answer is '9', so there is a tick in box A.
Now we are ready to start.
Look at question 1.
1   What is the man going to drink?
W: I'm thirsty. Let's go for a coffee.
M: I'd rather have a cold drink.
W: OK. Let's go to Kendon's. They have a really nice iced tea.
M: Actually, we don't have much time. Let's just get a bottle of water from the supermarket.
Narr: Now listen again.
2   What did the woman and her husband do on Friday?
M: So what did you do on Friday? Did you go to the theatre?
W: No, my husband and I wanted to go, but we couldn't get tickets.
M: Oh, what a pity. Did you stay at home?
W: Actually, there was a good film on at the cinema, so we went to see that instead.
Narr: Now listen again.
3   Where did the teacher spend last summer?
W: Your new teacher sounds really interesting
M: Yes, and she's lived in lots of different countries.
W: Really?
M: Yes, and she travels a lot, too. She spent the whole of last summer travelling around Australia, and next summer she's going to South America.
W: Wow! Has she ever been to the United States?
M: Yes, four times.
Narr: Now listen again.
4   Which subject does the man prefer?
M: The new maths teacher is really nice, isn't she?
W: She's okay, but maths is *not* my favourite subject. I like English best.
M: I don't. Our teacher is really strict. I like chemistry much more.
Narr: Now listen again.
5   Which shop will they go to next?
W: Well, I'm glad that's done! Thanks for coming. I couldn't have chosen a dress for the party by myself.
M: No problem. What else do we need to do?
W: Well, let's go and order the cake from the baker's now.
M: Good idea, and we can buy some paper plates from the supermarket on the way home.
Narr: Now listen again.
This is the end of Part 1.

Now look at Part 2.
Listen to Donna talking to Henry about painting her new flat.
What colours is Donna going to use?
For questions 6 – 10, write a letter (A – H) next to each part of the flat.
You will hear the conversation twice.

W: *(answering phone)* Hello?
M: Hi, Donna. It's Henry. I'm just calling to see how the move went. How's your new flat?
W: It's really nice, but it needs painting.
M: I could help you if you like. I'm free at the weekend.
W: Brilliant! The first thing that needs attention is the bathroom, as that's in the worst shape. The bath, sink and toilet are green, so I'm going to paint the walls yellow.
M: Listen. If you know what other colours you want, we can go and get the paint this afternoon.
W: That would be great! The walls in the entrance hall are a horrible shade of red at the moment and the front door is a dreadful grey. I want to paint the hall cream and the front door brown. Actually, I'm thinking of painting all the walls cream, except the kitchen and the dining room. I want to paint the kitchen blue.
M: What about the walls in the dining room?
W: They're purple at the moment, but I want to paint them a nice shade of green.
M: Okay ... and what about the ceilings?
W: The ceilings are all going to be white.
M: Okay. So . . . I'll pick you up this afternoon and we'll buy the paint. Is 2 o'clock all right?
W: Perfect! See you then!
Narr: Now listen again.
This is the end of Part 2.

Now look at Part 3.
Listen to Dawn asking about English Homestead Courses.
For questions 11 – 15, tick A, B or C.
You will hear the conversation twice.
Look at questions 11 – 15 now. You have 20 seconds.
Now listen to the conversation.
M: *(answering phone)* Hello, English Homestead Courses. Can I help you?
W: Hello. Can you tell me exactly what an English Homestead Course is, please?
M: Yes. If you take an English Homestead Course, you don't go to a school or college. You stay in your English teacher's home.
W: I see, but will I be able to meet any other students?
M: Yes, we get together with other students at the Sports Centre every Wednesday. And on Fridays we go to the cinema. Every Saturday we all go on an excursion together. Last week we went to London.
W: Do I need to take any books with me?
M: The only thing you need to take is a dictionary. We'll give you a course book and a grammar practice book when you get here.
W: Do you have courses in Scotland?
M: We have a few courses in Scotland and some in Wales but most of our courses are in England.
W: And how much do the courses cost?
M: A week-long course is £250, but if you take a four-week course, it costs only £860, which comes to £215 a week.
W: Does that include meals?
M: It includes meals, accommodation and lessons. The only thing you pay extra for is excursions.
W: Thanks for the information.
M: You're welcome.
Narr: Now listen again.
This is the end of Part 3.

Now look at Part 4.
You will hear a man booking a table at a restaurant.
Listen and complete questions 16 – 20. You will hear the conversation twice.
W: Good evening. This is Gino's. Can I help you?
M: It's my mother's birthday next week, so I'd like to book a table.

W: Certainly, sir. Which day is your mother's birthday on?

M: It's next Friday.

W: All right. Yes, that's Friday, 20th May. And how many people do you want to book the table for?

M: Let me see. *(thinking aloud)* There's my wife and I ... our two children ... and Mum, of course ... oh, and my brother James. So that's 6, isn't it?

W: It certainly is.

M: Well, I don't get home from work till 6 on Fridays, so let's say 7 o'clock.

W: And what would you like me to put on the cake?

M: Oh! I didn't know you did cakes, too! It's Mum's 70th birthday, but I think you'd better just put 'Happy Birthday'. I don't think she wants everyone to know her age!

W: That's fine. All I need now is your name.

M: Nick Sherman.

W: Sherman. Could you spell that, please?

M: Certainly. It's S – H – E – R – M – A – N.

W: Thank you, Mr Sherman. We'll see you on Friday.

Narr: Now listen again.
This is the end of Part 4.

Now look at Part 5.
You will hear some information about the Eastern Link Bus Service.
Listen and complete questions 21 – 25.
You will hear the information twice.

W: *(in style of recorded message)* Hello, and welcome to the Eastern Link Bus Service Information Line. Our buses will take you from your own home to local shops as well as to local coach and train stations.
The service operates every day, including weekends. Tickets are £1.50 for a single journey, and £2.50 for a return journey. To book your seat, just ring 0880 233 1888. That's 0880 233 1888. Simply leave your name, and tell us where you live and where you want to go. We recommend that you book your seat at least two hours before you want to travel.
You can also call into our offices to book your journey. We are located at 50 Station Road, just opposite the main bus station.
Thank you for calling the Eastern Link Bus Service Information Line.

Narr: Now listen again.
This is the end of Part 5. You now have 8 minutes to write your answers on the answer sheet.
[See page 157 for Listening Spotlight 1.]

TEST 2

Narr: This is the Cambridge Key English Test, Test 2, Paper 2. There are five parts to the test: Parts 1, 2, 3, 4 and 5. We will now stop for a moment before we start the test. Please ask any questions now because you mustn't speak during the test.
Now look at the instructions for Part 1.
You will hear five short conversations.
You will hear each conversation twice.
There is one question for each conversation.
For questions 1 – 5, put a tick under the right answer.
Here is an example:
How many students are there in the language class?

M: Are there many students in your language class?

W: There were ten, but one of them left.

M: That's quite a lot.

W: I know, but last year there were fifteen.

Narr: Now listen again.
The answer is '9', so there is a tick in box A.
Now we are ready to start.

Look at question 1.
1   Where is the hotel?

W: Excuse me. Can you tell me how to get to the Railway Hotel, please?

M: Yes, turn left at the traffic lights and you'll see it right next to the park.

W: Is it on the left or the right side of the street?

M: It's on the left.

Narr: Now listen again.
2   Where will Karen and Jim go at the weekend?

M: Hi, Karen. What are you and Jim going to do this weekend?

W: We're going swimming at that new hotel on the coast.

M: Are you going to swim in the outdoor pool?

W: No, it isn't open yet, so we'll swim in the indoor one.

Narr: Now listen again.
3   How much did the man's meal cost?

W: Was that new restaurant expensive, Dave?

M: It wasn't too bad. There were three of us, and the total bill came to £62.

W: That's quite a lot.

M: Steve and Larry paid £20 each, and I had the salmon, which was a little more expensive.

W: £22 for a meal is pretty expensive.

M: It was worth it, though. It's a fantastic restaurant.

Narr: Now listen again.
4   Where did David buy his trainers?

W: Great trainers, David. Where did you get them?

M: I looked everywhere – sports shops, the Internet – and I finally found a pair I liked at the street market.

W: Really? I didn't know they sold them there!

Narr: Now listen again.
5   What time does the circus start on Saturdays?

W: Did you see the advert in the newspaper about the circus?

M: No. When is it on?

W: It's at 7 pm on weekdays, 8 pm on Saturdays, and there's also an afternoon show at 3 pm on Sundays.

M: Great. Let's take the kids on Saturday.

Narr: Now listen again.
This is the end of Part 1.

Now look at Part 2.
Listen to Christine talking about her holiday.
Where did she spend each day?
For questions 6 – 10, write a letter (A – H) next to each day of the week.
You will hear the conversation twice.

M: Hello, Christine. You're looking great. How was your holiday?

W: Brilliant!

M: What did you do?

W: Well, we arrived on Monday morning and after we unpacked, we went on a trip to a Roman villa. You wouldn't believe some of the things there. The Romans were very clever people.

M: Yes, I remember our history teacher was always saying that. What did you do next?

W: Tuesday was a fun day. We went to a theme park. I didn't go on many of the rides, though. They were too frightening! Wednesday was my favourite day.

M: Let me guess: you spent it lying on a beach,

W: How did you know? Anyway, you're right. The next day we went to a carpet factory. The carpets were beautiful, but I felt sorry for the people who work there. They work very long hours.

M: Did you buy a carpet as a souvenir?

W: No, but a lot of people did. I bought my souvenirs on Friday at the local street market. They had some amazing things.

M: Yes. It's quite famous.

W: On the last day, <u>Saturday</u>, we had free time in the city centre. Some of the people in the group went to the museum and the art gallery. I decided to leave them for next time and I relaxed with a couple of new friends <u>in a coffee bar</u>.

M: Sounds great. Do you think Wendy would like it? We're planning to go somewhere in the summer.

W: She'll love it. I'll give you all the details when we meet up at the weekend.

Narr: Now listen again.
This is the end of Part 2.

Now look at Part 3.
Listen to a conversation in a ticket office.
For questions 11 – 15, tick A, B or C.
You will hear the conversation twice.
Look at questions 11 – 15 now. You have 20 seconds.
Now listen to the conversation.

W: Good morning. Can I help you?

M: Yes, I'd like to book some tickets for the international theatre festival.

W: Certainly, which plays are you interested in?

M: I'd like to see them all, especially the Greek play and the Italian one. But we can only come to the <u>French</u> one in the afternoon because my sister has a part-time job in the evenings.

W: I see. Well, we have afternoon performances on <u>Wednesday</u>. We used to have them on Saturday and Sunday, too, but we stopped doing that last year.

M: It will have to be Wednesday then.

W: Actually, there's also a special performance on <u>Wednesday morning at 10 am</u>, and the evening performance is a little earlier, too. It starts at 7 pm, not 7.30.

M: I can't come to that. I'm a student and I have lectures at the university in the mornings, and since my sister works in the evenings that <u>only leaves the afternoon.</u>

W: So, that's two tickets for the 3 pm performance then?

M: Yes. How much are the tickets?

W: They are £8 and £6.50. Is your sister a student, too?

M: Yes. Why do you ask?

W: Because we have a special offer for students. Tickets are <u>only £5</u> each.

M: Brilliant! Can I pay by credit card?

W: Certainly.

Narr: Now listen again.
This is the end of Part 3.

Now look at Part 4.
You will hear a woman asking for information about a computer.
Listen and complete questions 16 – 20.
You will hear the conversation twice.

M: *(answering phone)* Hello?

W: Hi! I'm calling about the computer you advertised in the *Evening News*. Is it a desktop computer or a laptop?

M: It's a laptop. I'm selling it because I've just bought a new desktop.

W: What colour is it?

M: It's really nice. It's black and <u>silver.</u>

W: And how much memory does it have?

M: It had 20 gigabytes when I bought it, but I made some changes and now it has <u>40</u> gigabytes.

W: Are there any accessories with it, like a mouse or headphones?

M: Yes, it comes with a mouse and a <u>microphone</u>, but it doesn't have headphones.

W: The advertisement said you were selling it with a carrying case. What's that like?

M: Well, it came with a metal carrying case, but I didn't like it. It was too heavy, so I bought one that's <u>black</u> <u>leather</u>. That's the one I'm selling it with.

W: And how much are you selling it for?

M: I advertised it for £500 last week, but nobody was interested, so now I'm selling it for <u>£425</u>. I'm a student, and I really need the money.

W: That's a good deal. Can I come and see it?

M: Of course. I'll be here all evening.

W: Great, I'll be there in about an hour.

M: See you soon.

Narr: Now listen again.
This is the end of Part 4.

Now look at Part 5.
You will hear some information about a special kind of sale at a department store.
Listen and complete questions 21 – 25.
You will hear the information twice.

M: *(in style of recording in department store lift)* Welcome to Sendal's fabulous 'Blue Cross Sale'. Remember, all items marked with a blue cross are <u>half</u> price at the moment. Not 10% less, not even 30% less, but a whole 50% less.
Don't miss our great bargains in all departments. For the fashion lovers among you, there's a fashion show on the second floor. The show takes place at <u>11</u> am and 3 pm daily, except <u>Thursdays</u>. There's also a daily cookery demonstration from 1 to 3 pm in the cookware section on the <u>third floor</u>.
And don't forget! The sale has been extended by one week but it finishes at the end of the <u>month</u>, so grab those bargains now!

Narr: Now listen again.
This is the end of Part 5. You now have 8 minutes to write your answers on the answer sheet.
[See page 157 for Listening Spotlight 2.]

TEST 3

Narr: This is the Cambridge Key English Test, Test 3, Paper 2. There are five parts to the test: Parts 1, 2, 3, 4 and 5. We will now stop for a moment before we start the test. Please ask any questions now because you mustn't speak during the test.
Now look at the instructions for Part 1.
You will hear five short conversations.
You will hear each conversation twice.
There is one question for each conversation.
For questions 1 – 5, put a tick under the right answer.
Here is an example:
How many students are there in the language class?

M: Are there many students in your language class?

W: There were ten, but one of them left.

M: That's quite a lot.

W: I know, but last year there were fifteen.

Narr: Now listen again
The answer is '9', so there is a tick in box A.
Now we are ready to start.
Look at question 1.
1 What will the weather be like at the weekend?

W: *(like a TV weather reporter)* And now for the weather forecast. The snow will continue until Wednesday. It will be windy and rainy on Thursday and Friday, but the good news is that there will be <u>clear skies and sunshine all over the country at the weekend.</u>

Narr: Now listen again.
2 Where do the man's parents live?

W: Where are your parents living now?

M: Well, they sold that lovely old house they had in London and moved to Madrid.

W: Really? Does either of them speak Spanish?

M: No, and that was a big problem, so they moved back to England last year and they're living in <u>Brighton</u> now.

Narr: Now listen again.

3   Which phone will the woman buy?

M: Can I help you?

W: Yes, I need a new phone.

M: You've come to the right place! We've got some great deals on mobile phones this week.

W: No, thanks, I've just bought a new mobile and I'm very pleased with it.

M: How about this new cordless phone? It's on sale at the moment.

W: No, I just want an <u>ordinary, old-fashioned phone</u>, please.

M: Of course. We have a wide choice just over here ...

Narr: Now listen again.

4   How will the man spend the evening?

W: Hello, Paul. How's that sister of mine keeping?

M: She's away for the weekend, visiting your parents.

W: Well, <u>a group of us are going to the new French restaurant in town</u>. Why don't you join us?

M: <u>That would be great.</u> I love going to restaurants, but I hate eating alone.

Narr: Now listen again.

5   How long will it take them to drive to the airport?

M: What time do we have to leave for the airport?

W: It depends on how you want to get there. The bus takes 90 minutes, and the train takes 40 minutes.

M: What about going by car?

W: That's probably a good idea. If we leave now, we'll be there in <u>an hour</u>.

Narr: Now listen again.
This is the end of Part 1.

Now look at Part 2.
Listen to Gerry and Penny planning a family trip to London. What place do they choose for each person to visit?
For questions 6 – 10, write a letter (A – H) next to each person.
You will hear the conversation twice.

W: Gerry, come and look at the information pack for our trip to London.

M: *(looking through the information)* There are so many things to do, Penny. I don't know where to start.

W: Well, why don't we start with the kids? I don't think Sally would like the zoo. She always feels sorry for the animals, but she's been asking about the London Eye for weeks, so we have to go there.

M: You're right. What about Billy? He loves boats, so it's either the Thames cruise or the zoo.

W: Definitely the <u>zoo for Billy</u>. What about an <u>opera at Covent Garden for your parents</u>?

M: <u>That would be great for Dad</u>, but <u>Mum would prefer to see a play at a West End theatre.</u>

W: I quite fancy one of the Thames cruises. It says here you can see the Houses of Parliament and the London Eye from the boat.

M: <u>So you don't want to go shopping in Oxford Street then?</u>

W: Which page is that on, Gerry? *(looking through information)* Wow! <u>This looks fantastic. There are so many great shops in Oxford Street. Will you come with me?</u>

M: I'll come if you really want me to, Penny, but <u>I'd much rather go to Madame Tussauds.</u>

W: *(laughing)* <u>Okay</u>, then!

Narr: Now listen again.
This is the end of Part 2.

Now look at Part 3.
Listen to Hillary asking for information about a gym.

For questions 11–15, tick A, B or C.
You will hear the conversation twice.
Look at questions 11– 15 now. You have 20 seconds.
Now listen to the conversation.

M: *(answering phone)* Hello. Shapers. Can I help you?

W: Oh, hi! I'd like some information about Shapers, please.

M: Well, I'll start with some background information so that you can see just how experienced Shapers is in the field of keeping fit. The first Shapers gym was opened in Manchester and gyms in London and Edinburgh followed after that. We now have half a million customers and thousands of gyms all over the world, including <u>155 in the UK</u>.

W: Wow! I didn't realise you were quite that big. Do you have a branch in Oldfield?

M: I'll just check for you. *(pause to check computer screen)*. I'm sure we do. Some of our gyms are in large hotels, others in shopping centres ... Ah, here we are. Yes, Shapers in Oldfield is in the Jardine <u>Shopping Centre</u>.

W: Really? That's great! I'm going to be working near there. What kinds of fitness programmes are available at Shapers?

M: Well, that's where we're different from most other gyms. <u>All our customers follow a specially designed programme using special equipment. No sweaty aerobics, no relaxing swimming pool.</u> It's hard work but if you follow the programme carefully, Shapers promises to get you fit and healthy.

W: That's interesting. What about the other members? How old are they?

M: All different ages. Anyone can join, as long as they bring a note from their doctor to say that they are healthy enough. We have programmes for children, teenagers and adults. Children aged 6 to 12 must be with an adult, and <u>anyone under 18 must have permission from their parents.</u>

W: When is Shapers open? I'd like to have a look around my local branch.

M: From 8 am to 10 pm. Actually, we have a special offer at the moment: a special one-day pass. <u>You can use it at any of the Shapers gyms in the UK. The only place you can't use it is the snack bar.</u> The snack bar is for members only.

W: That sounds great. Where can I get a pass?

M: Just call in at your local Shapers and ask for one.

W: Great. Thanks

M: You're welcome.

Narr: Now listen again.
This is the end of Part 3.

Now look at Part 4.
You will hear a woman ordering a pizza. Listen and complete questions 16 – 20. You will hear the conversation twice.

M: Good evening. Pizza Veneto.

W: Hello. I'd like to order two pizzas, please.

M: What kind would you like?

W: The one with ham, cheese, mushrooms and bacon. Is that the Royal?

M: No, the Royal has green pepper, too. The one you want is the <u>Special</u>. We have an offer at the moment. If you order two pizzas, we will give you either a third pizza or a salad free of charge.

W: Great. I think two pizzas is enough, so I'd like the <u>salad</u>, please.

M: Where would you like us to deliver the pizza?

W: <u>30</u> York Avenue.

M: Which floor?

W: <u>Fourth.</u>

M: And your name?

W: Doris Hough *(pronounced Huff)*. That's <u>H - O - U - G - H</u>.

M: Right then. Your pizzas will be there in about 20 minutes.
W: Thank you.
Narr: Now listen again.
This is the end of Part 4.

Now look at Part 5.
You will hear some information about a doctor's surgery.
Listen and complete questions 21 – 25.
You will hear the information twice.
W: Hello. Dr Alan Kindy's surgery. Can I help you?
M: Yes, I'm new to the area, and I would like some information about the surgery hours, please.
W: Certainly. The surgery is open from 8.30 am to <u>6.30</u> pm.
M: That's on weekdays, isn't it?
W: That's right: every day, <u>Monday to Friday</u>.
M: I have two young children, so I might need a doctor at weekends. What number should I ring?
W: The number to ring is <u>08198 655321</u>, and if it's an emergency, like a broken arm or leg, you can always go to the casualty department at <u>Eastside</u> General Hospital.
M: Just before we moved, I gave up smoking and I'm finding it really hard. Do you think that Dr Kindy will be able to suggest anything to help me? I'd hate to start again.
W: Yes, we have two clinics: a <u>stop smoking</u> clinic and a healthy heart clinic. You can get the details when you come to register.
M: That's fantastic! Thank you.
W: You're welcome.
Narr: Now listen again.
This is the end of Part 5. You now have 8 minutes to write your answers on the answer sheet.
[See page 157 for Listening Spotlight 3.]

TEST 4

Narr: This is the Cambridge Key English Test, Test 4, Paper 2. There are five parts to the test: Parts 1, 2, 3, 4 and 5. We will now stop for a moment before we start the test. Please ask any questions now because you mustn't speak during the test.
Now look at the instructions for Part 1.
You will hear five short conversations.
You will hear each conversation twice.
There is one question for each conversation.
For questions 1 – 5, put a tick under the right answer.
Here is an example:
How many students are there in the language class?
M: Are there many students in your language class?
W: There were ten, but one of them left.
M: That's quite a lot.
W: I know, but last year there were fifteen.
Narr: Now listen again
The answer is '9', so there is a tick in box A.
Now we are ready to start.
Look at question 1.
1 *How does Alan usually get to work?*
W: You're very late this morning, Alan.
M: I know. <u>I usually get the bus</u>, but I woke up late so I missed the bus ... *and* the train!
W: So how did you get here?
M: I had to phone for a taxi.
Narr: Now listen again
2 *Where will they go on their anniversary?*
M: What would you like to do on our anniversary?
W: Well, I don't want to go to the Italian restaurant again. The food wasn't very good last time.
M: How about the Chinese one, or the French one?
W: <u>Let's try the French one</u>. Sally went there last week. She said the food was delicious.

M: Okay.
Narr: Now listen again.
3 *What time will Frank arrive?*
W: What time are we meeting Frank tomorrow?
M: Well, he was going to catch the 9 am train, but he's got a class in the morning.
W: So which train is he going to catch?
M: He's going to catch the 1.30 train, <u>so he'll be here at 2.30.</u>
Narr: Now listen again.
4 *Which woman is Elaine's English teacher?*
M: Hey, Elaine! Isn't that your English teacher?
W: No, that woman has long straight blonde hair. My teacher has <u>medium-length, wavy blonde hair.</u>
Narr: Now listen again.
5 *How much did Brian pay for his jacket?*
W: Wow, I really like your jacket, Brian.
M: Thanks! I bought it in the sales.
W: Really? How much did you pay for it?
M: Well, it should have been £100, but it was reduced by £25, so <u>I only paid £75 for it.</u>
Narr: Now listen again.
This is the end of Part 1.

Now look at Part 2.
Listen to a couple talking about their friends' taste in films. Which kind of film does each of their friends like? For questions 6 – 10, write a letter (A – H) next to each person.
You will hear the conversation twice.
M: What shall we do tonight?
W: Why don't we invite a group of friends around to watch a DVD?
M: Good idea, but we need to choose one that everyone will like.
W: How about a thriller? It's always fun watching thrillers with friends.
M: Not with Adam. He hates them. Last time he watched a thriller, he couldn't sleep for days. He'd much rather watch a detective story.
W: Does John still like <u>science fiction films</u>?
M: <u>Yes</u>, but he doesn't get to watch them much anymore ... not since he married Jenny, that is. You know how it is: <u>Jenny's always preferred love stories.</u>
W: And what about <u>Dennis.</u> Doesn't he like science fiction, too?
M: <u>Not really. He prefers adventure films.</u>
W: Actually, one of the DVDs I was thinking of hiring is an adventure film. Do you think <u>Sally</u> would like it?
M: Only if it was based on a true story. Actually, she and Fred have been watching a lot of historical films lately. Fred's a historian, so he really loves them.
W: Oh, dear! I completely forgot about <u>Jane! She won't watch anything but documentaries,</u> so she won't like any of our suggestions.
M: This is much too difficult! Why don't we go to a disco on Saturday instead?
W: Now that's a great idea!
Narr: Now listen again.
This is the end of Part 2.

Now look at Part 3.
Listen to Pauline talking to a man in a shop about some furniture she has ordered. For questions 11 – 15, tick A, B or C. You will hear the conversation twice.
M: Good morning. Can I help you?
W: You certainly can. I have a complaint about some furniture I ordered.
M: Oh, dear. We've had a lot of problems with orders made on our websites and over the phone recently.
W: Actually, I came in and ordered it straight from the shop.
M: Oh. When did you order the furniture?

Audioscript

W: Well, I ordered it on <u>Monday</u>, and you said it would be delivered on Tuesday. It arrived on Thursday.

M: I'm afraid that happens sometimes. I'm very sorry about the late delivery.

W: It wasn't just a late delivery. There was a problem with the furniture, too.

M: What exactly did you order?

W: The Regency dining table and six chairs.

M: The Regency dining suite comes in brown, black and white. Which colour did you order?

W: I ordered the brown one, but <u>a black dining table was delivered</u>.

M: Ah, I remember now. We don't have any brown ones in stock.

W: Yes, but <u>the chairs you sent were brown.</u>

M: Oh, dear. I'm terribly sorry! <u>Would you like me to arrange for the black chairs to be delivered?</u> Our delivery company could bring them to you tomorrow.

W: *(noticeably irritated)* I most certainly would not! I ordered a brown dining suite because that's what I wanted. I'm not interested in a black one. <u>What I want is my money back!</u>

M: I understand completely. Could you wait a moment? I'll have to speak to the manager about a refund.

Narr: Now listen again.
This is the end of Part 3.

Now look at Part 4.
You will hear a man registering with an employment agency.
Listen and complete questions 16 to 20.
You will hear the conversation twice.

W: Good morning. How can I help you?

M: I'm looking for a job.

W: Great! I'll just need a few details. First of all, what kind of job: part-time or holiday?

M: Holiday.

W: Okay, now I'll need your name, please.

M: John Sheridan.

W: Is that <u>S-H-E-R-I-D-A-N</u>?

M: Yes, that's right.

W: And your address?

M: <u>30</u> London Road.

W: And your phone number?

M: <u>0116 310 2538.</u>

W: Now, John, what kind of work are you looking for?

M: Maybe a clerk in an office, or a <u>shop assistant</u>.

W: And how much do you want to earn?

M: I'm not really trained for anything, so I'm expecting the minimum wage. It's <u>£5.50</u> per hour, isn't it?

W: Yes, that's right. Well, John, I have all your details, so I'll call you as soon as we find a job for you.

M: Thank you.

Narr: Now listen again.
This is the end of Part 4.

Now look at Part 5
You will hear some information about something that was found on a bus.
Listen and complete questions 21 – 25.
You will hear the information twice.

M: *(in the style of a radio broadcaster)* And finally on this morning's show, we have a report of a book that was found on a bus. The book was found on the Number <u>17</u> bus, which operates between Ashton and the city centre. The bus left <u>Ashton Bus Station</u> at <u>20 past 8</u> this morning. When it arrived in the city centre, the driver found a <u>paperback</u> book on one of the seats. The title of the book is *French for Beginners*. So if you think you might have left your book on the bus this morning, call the bus station now.

Narr: Now listen again.
This is the end of Part 5. You now have 8 minutes to write your answers on the answer sheet.
[See page 158 for Listening Spotlight 4.]

TEST 5

Narr: This is the Cambridge Key English Test, Test 5, Paper 2. There are five parts to the test: Parts 1, 2, 3, 4 and 5. We will now stop for a moment before we start the test. Please ask any questions now because you mustn't speak during the test.
Now look at the instructions for Part 1.
You will hear five short conversations.
You will hear each conversation twice.
There is one question for each conversation.
For questions 1 – 5, put a tick under the right answer.
Here is an example:
How many students are there in the language class?

M: Are there many students in your language class?

W: There were ten, but one of them left.

M: That's quite a lot.

W: I know, but last year there were fifteen.

Narr: Now listen again
The answer is '9', so there is a tick in box A.
Now we are ready to start.
Look at question 1.
1   Which table does the man like?

W: Good morning. Can I help you?

M: Yes, I'm looking around for a table.

W: Have you seen anything you like?

M: Well, I saw one in the window that's really nice.

W: The square dining table with the chairs around it?

M: No, the <u>small rectangular coffee table.</u>

Narr: Now listen again.
2   What time does Mary's party start?

M: Are you going to Mary's party on Saturday?

W: It starts <u>at 8 o'clock</u>, doesn't it?

M: <u>Yes</u>, she was going to have it later at 9, but she changed her mind.

W: I'm glad she did. I've arranged for Jim to pick me up at 7.30.

Narr: Now listen again.
3   Where will Tina go on holiday?

W: Hi! Have you heard the news? Tina won first prize in a competition.

M: Wow! What did she win?

W: A free holiday for two people.

M: In Europe, or anywhere in the world?

W: Anywhere! <u>She's chosen Australia</u>.

M: I'm surprised she didn't choose Austria. Her brother lives there, doesn't he?

W: Yes, but she's been there four times already.

Narr: Now listen again.
4   What has the man lost?

W: You look like you've lost something. What are you looking for?

M: *(emptying out his pockets)* Gloves, ... bus tickets, ...change ... No, everything's here except what I need.

W: And what's that?

M: My favourite <u>pen</u>! I had it a few minutes ago, but it seems to have disappeared!

W: Never mind. I've got a spare one you can borrow. Here!

Narr: Now listen again.
5   How much does one ticket cost?

W: *(at a theatre box office)* Can I help you?

M: Yes, I'd like five tickets for Saturday's performance, please.

W: <u>They're £15 each</u>, which comes to £75.

M: Oh, dear! I haven't got that much with me. I thought student tickets cost 50% less?

W: Not for this performance, I'm afraid.

M: Can I pay by credit card?

W: Yes, of course.

Audioscript

Narr: Now listen again.
This is the end of Part 1.

Now look at Part 2.
Listen to Anita talking to John about shopping.
What is John going to buy from each shop?
For questions 6 – 10, write a letter (A – H) next to each shop.
You will hear the conversation twice.
(phone rings)

M: *(answering the phone)* Hello? ... Oh, hi, Anita. How's your leg?

W: It's a lot better, but the doctor says I shouldn't go out yet. That's why I'm calling. Can you do some shopping for me?

M: No problem. I'm going to the shops this afternoon. What do you need?

W: Can you get me a new bandage for my leg? Oh, ... and some toothpaste.

M: Of course! Both from the chemist's?

W: No, you can get the bandage at the chemist, but I always buy my toothpaste from the supermarket. It's much cheaper there.

M: Okay. What else?

W: Will you be going to the baker's?

M: Yes. Do you need bread?

W: No, but I do need a birthday cake. It's Ray's birthday on Sunday. Oh, and can you get some wrapping paper from the newsagent's?

M: You'll need a card, too, won't you?

W: No, I've already bought one, but could you go to the butcher's for me? I thought I'd invite you and Vera for Sunday lunch. What shall I cook? Chicken ... or lamb?

M: I like both, but Vera prefers chicken, so why don't you do that? I need to go to the greengrocer's for some fruit and vegetables and there's a new butcher's shop right next door! I can buy a chicken from there!

W: Good idea. I really appreciate your help.

M: No problem. That's what friends are for!

Narr: Now listen again.
This is the end of Part 2.

Now look at Part 3.
Listen to George asking about computer courses.
For questions 11 – 15, tick A, B or C.
You will hear the conversation twice.
Look at questions 11 – 15 now. You have 20 seconds.
Now listen to the conversation.

M: Hello. I'd like to sign up for a computer course.

W: What kind of course are you interested in: a beginners course, like how to send and receive e-mails; a more advanced course, like using the Internet for research; or a professional course, like website design?

M: I think I'd better start with the first one. How many people will there be in the class?

W: We realise that students who are not used to computers need a lot of help, so we never have more than four students in our beginners classes. The more advanced and professional classes have between six and ten students.

M: When are the classes?

W: We have classes every weekday from 9 am to 12 pm, and on Wednesdays there are classes from 5 pm to 8 pm, too.

M: And how long is the course?

W: 60 hours. Each lesson is three hours, and there are lessons every day, so it takes four weeks to complete the course.

M: That's quite a lot of hours. What do the lessons cost?

W: We charge £3 per lesson. Actually we have a special offer on at the moment. If you pay for the whole course when you enrol, it's only £42, instead of £60.

M: Brilliant. Can I enrol today?

W: Yes, we're open from 9 am to 5 pm, but if you don't have much time, I suggest you come after lunch. The office gets very busy in the mornings.

M: Okay. I'll call in around 2 pm.

W: That's great. I look forward to seeing you.

Narr: Now listen again.
This is the end of Part 3.

Now look at Part 4.
You will hear a man booking a taxi. Listen and complete questions 16 – 20. You will hear the conversation twice.

W: Good morning. Bradford Cabs.

M: Good morning. My name is Bill Lanford, and I'd like to book a taxi.

W: Certainly. When do you want to book it for?

M: Tuesday ... No, sorry. Thursday, 26th June.

W: At what time?

M: My flight is at 8 am, so let's say 5.30.

W: That doesn't give you much time to get to the airport. You need to check in 2 hours before the flight.

M: Really? How about 5 o'clock then?

W: Yes, that should give you enough time. Where would you like the taxi to pick you up from?

M: 16 Manshaw Road. That's Manshaw, M - A - N - S - H - A - W, number 16.

W: Got it. That's near the railway station, isn't it?

M: Yes, that's right.

W: And which terminal does your flight leave from?

M: Terminal 2 ... and, of course, that's Manchester Airport.

W: I just need your phone number now.

M: Of course. It's 310 1408.

W: OK. That's 310 1408.

M: Yes, that's correct.

W: Thank you. The driver will call you when he's on his way.

M: Okay, thanks. Bye.

Narr: Now listen again.
This is the end of Part 4.

Now look at Part 5.
You will hear some information about an excursion.
Listen and complete questions 21 – 25.
You will hear the information twice.

W: Welcome to the hotel. I hope you all had a good journey. Before you all go to dinner, I would just like to give you some information about the Roman Villa and Gardens. You may have read in your guidebooks that the Villa is closed on Sundays, but from tomorrow, the Villa will be open every day from 10 am to 5 pm. There is a lot to see at the Roman site, so I really do recommend that you take the guided tour. The tour leaves from outside the Villa entrance, but you need to go into the main building to book a ticket for the tour. The last guided tour is at 4 pm, one hour before closing time. If you don't want to take the guided tour, you may explore the grounds by yourself. Admission is free of charge: it doesn't cost anything. The cost of the tour is £4.50, but it really is worth every penny. If anyone would like more information about the Roman Villa or any of our other excursions, I will be in the reception area every morning after breakfast. Enjoy your stay!

Narr: Now listen again.
This is the end of Part 5. You now have 8 minutes to write your answers on the answer sheet.
[See page 158 for Listening Spotlight 5.]

Test 6

Narr: This is the Cambridge Key English Test, Test 6, Paper 2.

Audioscript

There are five parts to the test: Parts 1, 2, 3, 4 and 5. We will now stop for a moment before we start the test. Please ask any questions now because you mustn't speak during the test.

Now look at the instructions for Part 1.
You will hear five short conversations.
You will hear each conversation twice.
There is one question for each conversation.
For questions 1 – 5, put a tick under the right answer.
Here is an example:
How many students are there in the language class?

M: Are there many students in your language class?
W: There were ten, but one of them left.
M: That's quite a lot.
W: I know, but last year there were fifteen.
Narr: Now listen again.
The answer is '9', so there is a tick in box A.
Now we are ready to start.
Look at question 1.
1 What is the man going to do at the weekend?
W: Hi, Ken! Are you coming to Sally's party on Saturday?
M: Haven't you heard? My mum was in hospital all last week.
W: Oh dear! Is she okay now?
M: Yes, she is, but I'm staying with her until Dad gets back on Monday.
Narr: Now listen again.
2 How much did the woman's ticket cost?
M: Hello, Mary. Listen, I have to fly to Paris next weekend and you travel often. How much do you think the ticket will cost?
W: I went a couple of weeks ago, and I paid £120: that's £60 each way.
M: That sounds very reasonable.
W: Yes, it was a special offer for the bank holiday. The usual price is about £180.
Narr: Now listen again.
3 What are they going to have for dinner?
W: Do you fancy a salad for dinner tonight?
M: Sounds good. Shall I cook some steaks to go with it? I'm really hungry.
W: That'll take too long, won't it? There's some ham in the fridge, and we've got plenty of cheese.
M: No, it won't take long at all. How would you like yours?
W: Well done, please!
M: Okay! Two steaks coming up!
Narr: Now listen again.
4 What kind of mirror is the woman looking for?
M: Hi, Zoe. How are you?
W: Fine, thanks. I wonder if you could come to the shops with me this afternoon. I'm looking for a big square mirror for my bathroom.
M: Have you seen anything you like?
W: So far I've only found round ones and diamond-shaped ones, but they're not what I'm looking for.
Narr: Now listen again.
5 What time is the first train to London?
W: Hello. Can you tell me the time of the first train to London tomorrow morning, please?
M: Certainly, ma'am. It leaves at 5.15 from Platform 15.
W: Thank you.
Narr: Now listen again.
This is the end of Part 1.

Now look at Part 2.
Listen to Will talking to Katherine about the gifts she bought in a charity shop.
Who got which gift?
For questions 6 – 10, write a letter (A – H) next to each person.
You will hear the conversation twice.

W: Have you been to the new charity shop on Castle Street yet? It's amazing. There's so much great stuff there! I bought gifts for everyone!
M: Really? What did you buy?
W: Well, Irene was the easiest.
M: Oh, yes! She loves clothes. Did you get her a T-shirt?
W: Well, I thought about that, but they weren't her style; they had pictures of animals on them. I got her a great hat, though.
M: Mick likes pictures of animals. Did you get him a T-shirt?
W: No, I got him a poster of a tiger for his new flat. It has the same picture as the cup I bought for his girlfriend June.
M: What did you get for Anne?
W: I couldn't decide whether to get her a calendar or a diary. In the end I got her a calendar with pictures of endangered animals. I did buy the diary, though. I'm going to give it to Sarah.
M: That only leaves Tom and me. I hope you got him a pen. He borrowed mine last week and he still hasn't given it back to me!
W: No, they didn't have any, so I got him a sketchpad. He'll be able to use it in his art classes.
M: What about me?
W: Sorry, I didn't have enough money to get you anything. ... (chuckling) No, just joking. Here, this is for you.
M: (pausing, as if opening a gift) It's beautiful. Thank you!
Narr: Now listen again.
This is the end of Part 2.

Now look at Part 3.
Listen to a tour guide talking to a woman tourist about a local market.
For questions 11 – 15, tick A, B or C.
You will hear the conversation twice.
Look at questions 11 – 15 now. You have 20 seconds.
Now listen to the conversation.
W: My husband and I are going off to Ashbridge Market this morning. Could you tell me about it?
M: Of course! It's one of my favourites! Ashbridge is actually one of the oldest markets in England. Believe it or not, it began in 1289, and in 1869 an indoor market hall was built. In 1960, a car park was added, but there's been nothing else added since then...except more and more vendors, of course. It's a very popular place!
W: Goodness, I hadn't realised the indoor market was relatively new. What did the people do when the weather was very hot or very cold? What about when it rained?
M: Don't forget that we don't often have very hot weather in England, and the winters are usually quite mild. According to our records, the market didn't open when it was raining.
W: Is the market open every day now?
M: No, it's closed on Sundays. There are two special markets: a flea market every Tuesday, which sells used goods at very low prices ... and a European market every Friday, where you can buy foods from other European countries. There's an ordinary market on the other four days.
W: What if we get hungry or thirsty after all that shopping?
M: I'm glad you asked. There are several good coffee bars and tea rooms in the market hall. Most of them sell sandwiches and cakes. If you want a hot meal, there's a good choice of restaurants in the shopping centre nearby. Is there anything else I can help you with?
W: No, you've been very helpful! Thank you so much!
Narr: Now listen again.
This is the end of Part 3.

Now look at Part 4.
You will hear a man registering as a volunteer. Listen and complete questions 16 – 20. You will hear the conversation twice.
W: Good morning, Keep Britain Clean.

M: Yes, hello. I'd like to volunteer for the 'Clean Up the Park' project.

W: Great. Now I'll just need a couple of details before I tell you about the project. First, can I have your name, please?

M: Certainly. It's John Phillips, That's John, J – O – H – N, (pause) Phillips, P – H – I – double L – I – P – S.

W: And a phone number, in case we need to contact you?

M: My home number is 310 1714, but I'm usually out during the day, so I'll give you my mobile phone number. It's 0770 234 5115.

W: That's fine. Now, all volunteers must be at least 18. How old are you?

M: I'll be 19 next month.

W: Fine! And are you available on weekdays?

M: I'm afraid not. I'm free every weekend, though.

W: That's fine. And how will you be getting to the park. Do you have your own car?

M: No. Is that a problem?

W: Not at all. There's a free bus to and from the park, and we can arrange for you to take it. It leaves from outside our office at 8 am on Saturday and Sunday.

M: Great! Thank you very much. I guess I'll see you on Saturday at 8!

W: You're welcome. Thank you for volunteering!

Narr: Now listen again
This is the end of Part 4.

Now look at Part 5.
You will hear some information about a recording studio. Listen and complete questions 21 – 25. You will hear the information twice.

W: (recorded message) Hello, and welcome to Annex Recording Studio. Conveniently situated near the town centre at 199 Oxford Road, Annex Recording Studio offers all the facilities you would expect from a professional recording studio, including the hire of keyboards, guitars and drums, if you need them. To book, just complete the online booking form on our website. Please note that the minimum booking is one hour, and our rate is just £35 an hour. The studio also has a small coffee bar serving drinks and snacks all day long ... *[fade out]*

Narr: Now listen again.
This is the end of Part 5. You now have 8 minutes to write your answers on the answer sheet.
[See page 158 for Listening Spotlight 6.]

Listening Spotlights

Listening Spotlight 1

Listen to a man talking to a travel agent. For items 1 to 8, write the words the man spells. You will hear each item twice.

1 **W:** Could I have your last name, please?
   M: Yes, of course. It's Campbell.
   W: Could you spell that for me?
   M: Certainly. It's Campbell. That's C – A – M – P – B – E – double L.
   W: Got it.

2 **W:** Now, could I have your first name?
   M: Sure. It's Graham. That's G – R – A – H – A – M.

3 **W:** And I'll need your wife's name, too.
   M: Okay. It's Yvonne. Y – V – O – double N – E.

4 **W:** And your daughter's name?
   M: Elizabeth. E – L – I – Z – A – B – E – T – H.

5 **W:** Could you give me your address, please?
   M: Certainly. 44 Judgement Way. That's two words:Judgement, J – U – D – G – E – M – E – N –T, and Way, W – A – Y.

6 **W:** And which town do you live in?
   M: Exeter. E – X – E – T – E – R.

7 **W:** And could I have your post code, please?
   M: Yes. It's EQ1 4FK.

8 **W:** OK, we're almost done. Last question. What's your place of birth?
   M: Didcot, D – I – D – C – O – T.
   W: Great. I've got everything I need. Thanks!

Listening Spotlight 2

For items 1 to 3, write the phone numbers you hear. You will hear each item twice.

1 **W:** My home phone number is 235 7557.
2 **M:** My mobile phone number is 0747 126 9005.

3 **W:** To find out more, call our information line on 0800 153 4444.

In items 4 to 8, underline the number you hear. You will hear each item twice.

4 **M:** Good morning, everyone. We'll begin our tour today with a visit to the palace, which was built in the year 960.

5 **W:** The next train to leave from platform 5 will be the 15.50 service to London Euston.

6 **M:** Welcome to the UK cycling tour. During the next fourteen days, we will cover a distance of 818 miles, and visit many of the most popular sights in the British Isles ... *(fade out)*

7 **W:** ...and don't miss today's special offer. All tennis shoes are reduced to £19.90. Hurry!

8 **M:** The first episode of this popular series will be repeated on 13th June at ... *(fade out)*

Follow-Up: Now work with a partner. Take turns reading the numbers in the exercise.

Listening Spotlight 3

For items 1 to 6, read the questions and underline the key words. Then listen to the speakers and fill in the correct numbers. You will hear each item twice.

1 **W:** Flight BA70 to Paris is boarding at Gate 17 in 15 minutes.

2 **M:** Tickets cost £3.50 for adults, £1.50 for students and £1.00 for pensioners.

3 **W:** The centre is open from 9 am to 5 pm Monday to Friday, 9 am to 8 pm on Saturdays and 10 am to 2 pm on Sundays.

4 **M:** We have to be at the airport by 10.40 because our flight leaves at 12.40, so that means we'd better leave the house at 10.

5 **W:** We were planning to go to the cinema at 1.30, but John had to work until 6.30, so <u>we went at 7.30.</u>

6 **M:** It takes me <u>an hour</u> to get home, unless I leave late; then it takes an hour and a half, but yesterday there was so much traffic it took me over two hours!

Listening Spotlight 4

Read each question and underline the key words. Then listen to each speaker and underline the answer. You will hear each item twice.

1 **Listen to a man and woman talking about their holiday.**
  W: I'm really looking forward to our holiday. Where did you say we were going first?
  M: Italy, and we've got a very busy schedule. We visit Venice on Monday, <u>Pisa on Wednesday</u> and Rome on Friday.

2 **Listen to a man talking to a shop assistant.**
  M: Hello! I'm looking for a present for my son's 12th birthday. He hates reading and he never writes anything, except on his computer.
  W: <u>How about a CD?</u> We have a music department with a fantastic selection.
  M: <u>Brilliant idea!</u> Where's the music department?

3 **Listen to a woman asking a tour guide for information.**
  W: Hi! Can you give me some more information about tomorrow's tour, please?
  M: Of course. We start with a visit to the museum, then the castle gardens – they really are quite amazing! Our final stop will be a tour of the <u>castle</u> itself.

4 **Listen to a woman talking to her travel agent about a hotel booking.**
  W: Hello, Mr Granger. I'm just calling to ask which hotel you booked me into.
  M: Well, I thought about the Imperial. It really is very nice, but it doesn't have a car park. Then I considered the Palace, which has a car park, but it doesn't have a restaurant. So, finally, I booked you into <u>the Midland</u>.

5 **Listen to a man and a woman talking about a friend's birthday party.**
  M: Is Alan's birthday on Saturday?
  W: No. it's on <u>Thursday</u>. Most of us have to get up early on Friday morning though, so he's having the party on Saturday.

6 **Listen to a woman talking to a travel agent about her next holiday.**
  M: Where would you like to go? We have some great offers on at the moment.
  W: Well, I went to Greece last year and France the year before, so I'd like to do something different this year. Do you have any brochures about skiing holidays in <u>Austria</u>?

Listening Spotlight 5

Listen to each speaker and fill in the missing information. You will hear each item twice.

1 **M:** We have two restaurants and a snack bar which sells <u>sandwiches</u> throughout the day.

2 **W:** Welcome to the Alpha Language Centre Information Line. Alpha offers a wide range of courses in French, Spanish and German. Our next round of courses starts on <u>February</u> 13th. If you would like to register, please hold the line and ... *(fade out)*

3 **M:** Hi, Mary. You're not home so I'm leaving you a voice mail. I'm running a bit late, so I can't pick you up tonight. Please meet me at the <u>theatre</u>. See you later!

4 **W:** Hello. I have a problem I'm hoping you can help me with. I bought a <u>DVD player</u> from your shop yesterday, but I'm afraid the instruction book is missing.

5 **M:** Wexbridge Planning Department is closed on <u>Saturdays</u>. Our hours of operation are 9 am to 5 pm, Monday to Friday.

6 **W:** I'm pleased to announce that Val Jones will be the instructor for our next tennis course, which starts in <u>October</u> 2006.

7 **M:** That's right. I've been living here for over a year now. I moved here last <u>winter</u>.

8 **W:** For a starter? Let me see ... Yes, I think I'll have <u>chicken soup</u>, please. And then for the main course, I'd like ... *(fade out)*

Listening Spotlight 6

Listen to a man and woman arranging a delivery. Fill in the form. The conversation is in two parts. You will hear each part twice.

Part 1
M: Good afternoon. I'd like to send this package, please. Can you help me?
W: Of course. I'll just need a few details for the delivery. Who would you like the package delivered to?
M: Jennings Motors. That's <u>J – E – double N – I – N – G – S</u>.
W: Thanks, and the address?
M: <u>11 Station Road.</u>
W: Can you give me a contact name at the company, please?
M: That would be Eric George. No, wait a minute. Eric's on holiday this month. Now I remember. Tom's dealing with deliveries at the moment. <u>Tom Smith.</u>
W: Got it. And what day would you like the package delivered?
M: Well, today is Friday, and Monday is a bank holiday, so <u>Tuesday</u> would be fine.

Part 2
W: Now just a few more details. What time would you like the package delivered?
M: <u>Before 12 noon,</u> if possible. They open at 9.
W: Fine, I'll make a note of that. And could I have your name?
M: Certainly. It's Wally Weymouth. Let me spell that for you. Wally, <u>W – A – double L – Y.</u> Weymouth, <u>W – E – Y – M – O – U – T - H.</u>
W: And a contact phone number?
M: Yes, I'll give you my mobile. It's <u>0778 312 5469</u>.
W: Thanks. That will be £5.15, please.
M: Here you are.
W: Thank you.

HEINLE
CENGAGE Learning

Cambridge KET Practice Tests
by Dorothy Adams, with Diane Flanel Piniaris

Acknowledgements

The publishers would like to thank Visual Hellas for permission to reproduce copyright photographs.

PET answer sheets reprinted with the permission of University of Cambridge ESOL Examinations, Cambridge, England.

Illustrations by Theofanis Skafidas

Recording at GFS-PRO Studio by George Flamouridis

© 2006 New Editions, a part of Cengage Learning

ALL RIGHTS RESERVED. No part of this work covered by the copyright herein may be reproduced, transmitted, stored, or used in any form or by any means graphic, electronic, or mechanical, including but not limited to photocopying, recording, scanning, digitizing, taping, Web distribution, information networks, or information storage and retrieval systems, without the prior written permission of the publisher.

For permission to use material from this text or product, submit all requests online at **www.cengage.com/permissions**
Further permissions questions can be emailed to
permissionrequest@cengage.com

ISBN: 978-960-403-427-7

Cengage Learning EMEA
Cheriton House
North Way
Andover
Hampshire
SP10 5BE
United Kingdom

Cengage Learning is a leading provider of customized learning solutions with office locations around the globe, including Singapore, the United Kingdom, Australia, Mexico, Brazil and Japan. Locate your local office at:
international.cengage.com/region

Cengage Learning products are represented in Canada by Nelson Education, Ltd.

Visit Heinle online at **elt.heinle.com**
Visit our corporate website at **www.cengage.com**

Printed in the United Kingdom by Lightning Source
Print Number 05 Print Year 2016

www.ingramcontent.com/pod-product-compliance
Ingram Content Group UK Ltd.
Pitfield, Milton Keynes, MK11 3LW, UK
UKHW052247270225
455668UK00008B/45